MAKING ROOM FOR
Katherine

PHILIPPA GREENE MULFORD

MAKING ROOM FOR
Katherine

Macmillan Publishing Company   New York

Maxwell Macmillan Canada   Toronto

Maxwell Macmillan International
New York   Oxford   Singapore   Sydney

First edition. Printed in the United States of America

10 9 8 7 6 5 4 3 2 1

The text of this book is set in 13 point Garamond No. 3.

Library of Congress Cataloging-in-Publication Data
Mulford, Philippa Greene.
  Making room for Katherine / by Philippa Greene Mulford. — 1st ed.
    p. cm.
  Sequel to: The world is my eggshell.
  Summary: While trying to deal with the possibility that their mother may remarry, sixteen-year-old Abbey and her brother and sister are changed by a visit from their sophisticated thirteen-year-old cousin Katherine.
  ISBN 0-02-767652-8
  [1. Cousins—Fiction. 2. Brothers and sisters—Fiction. 3. Remarriage—Fiction.] I. Title.   PZ7.M895Mak 1994   [Fic]—dc20   93-32268

For L. A. M.

One

"Now, Abbey," Joyce soothed from the other side of the closet door, "it can't be *that* short."

"That's what you think!" I wailed. "My head feels like a *coconut*."

There was a burst of laughter, followed by Shel telling Joyce, "You got to admit that paints quite a picture." He pounded on the door. "Quit acting like an idiot and come out of there, Abbey!"

"No! I am never coming out of here again. I am never going to forgive Katherine for this haircut either!"

"That's not fair," my little sister said.

"Joyce is right, Ab," Shel agreed. "You were the one who asked Katherine to cut your hair."

I sighed, putting my chin in my hand. It was true. I had hoped that if I got my hair cut ultrashort like my cousin Katherine's, it might make me look suave and sophisticated. Like my cousin Katherine. Another dream bites the dust, I thought sadly.

Katherine had lived a "rarefied existence," as my mother put it. For one thing, she'd grown up in Paris, France, because her mother, my aunt Claudia, was a freelance writer. Mom said Katherine lived

with various friends' families while her mother trav-
eled, pursuing stories.

No wonder my cousin was one hundred times
more sophisticated than I was, I thought, even
though she was only thirteen, *eons* younger.

I ran a hand over my nearly bald head, asking,
"What am I going to *do,* you guys?"

"You're going to come out of that closet before I
take the door off the hinges," said Sheldon.

I gasped. "You wouldn't *dare.*"

"You know better than that, Ab," said Joyce. Shel
broke up.

She was right, of course. My twin would like
nothing better than an excuse to get out Dad's tool-
box and start monkeying around with the closet
door. The next thing you'd know, he'd louse it up,
and Mom would have to hire someone to repair the
damage. The last thing we needed around here was
another bill.

"All right, you bozo," I snapped. "I'll come out!
But you have to *promise* you won't laugh. I mean it,
Sheldon!"

There was a brief pause. Then, "Just how short is
your hair, Ab?"

I sighed. "It's so short . . . a baby porcupine would
come up to me and say, 'Hi, Mom.'" They burst out
laughing. In fact, my brother and sister sounded as
if they might hurt themselves, rolling around like
that. "Woe is me," I groaned. "Not only am I ruined
for life, but tomorrow I start baby-sitting the Costel-

lo kids at their club." Where Rick Risteen works as a lifeguard, I added silently.

Rick was the big brother of a girl I knew at school. He was tall, dark, and a freshman in college. Earlier, while I was still your basic all-American type with shoulder-length, streaky blond hair, I had probably had the ghost of a chance with a boy like Rick.

Now, in my new disguise as a coconut, he'd never give me the time of day. My life was over, my future black, my . . .

There was a rap on the closet door. "Hurry and come out!" Joyce ordered. "We just heard Katherine come in. You can't let her find you hiding in there."

"Remember what Mom told us, Ab," Shel prompted.

The night before Katherine arrived last week, Mom instructed us to be extra kind to our cousin. She said that Aunt Claudia was "between jobs," so she'd sent Katherine to us for the summer while she looked for work. Considering Katherine didn't live with her mother anyway, this didn't make complete sense to me, but Mom looked kind of upset, so I tried not to ask too many questions.

Especially when Mom said, "Put yourself in Katherine's shoes, kids. Imagine how you'd feel if *I* was out of work and I sent you off to relatives."

Shel and I had exchanged a look. Without saying a word, we knew that we simply couldn't imagine that. Later, Shel told me, "Mom would never do that to us, no matter what."

Now Joyce said, "She's on her way upstairs, Abbey!"

I scrambled to my feet and unlocked the closet door. Taking a deep breath, I stepped out into the light and—

"*Boy!*" said Joyce.

"Jeez," Shel whispered. Turning to Joyce, he added, "Her head *does* look like a coconut."

They circled me. Finally, Joyce stopped in front of me. "It's not that it's not a great haircut, Ab. . . ."

"I know. It's just not . . . me."

"On the other hand," Shel asked, "what *is?*" He mimed breaking up just as our cousin walked into the room.

She started to smile, then looked at me. "Have you been crying, Abbey?"

"Who, me?" I sniffled.

"Nice scalp job, Katherine," Shel chortled. "Just kidding," he added when she looked stricken.

"But she said she wanted her hair cut just like mine," Katherine told him.

"And I did, I did!" I assured her. "It's just such a . . . *change,* and I've never been too good about change. . . ."

"Understatement of the week, man!" Shel laughed.

I shot him a look as I patted Katherine's shoulder. "Don't worry. I wanted it this short. . . . I just didn't realize how much it would make my face stand out," I added, sending Sheldon staggering around, bumping into the bunk bed, laughing like the dyed-in-the-wool maniac he was. Raising my voice above the cacophony, I went on, "Keep in mind that hair grows back. . . ."

"We *hope*, anyway!" Shel crowed. I lunged at him, and he shot out of the room.

After slamming the door after him, Joyce blew her wispy blond hair out of her face. "He is such a pain. I don't know how we *stand* him."

"We don't," I said, and Katherine burst out laughing. "Don't tell me you think Sheldon's *funny*."

"I do. . . . I can't help it," she said, wiping her eyes. "I love how you three treat each other."

"Not really," Joyce said, incredulous.

Katherine nodded. "It's so real."

"It's that, all right," I agreed.

"Anyone like to play double solitaire with me?" Katherine asked, carefully making her way between the bunks and my bed to get to the window seat.

"I will," Joyce answered. "Excuse me, Ab."

I sat down on the bed so that she could get the deck of cards from the top of the bureau. This room was small when it was just Joyce and me. Now, with three of us sharing it, it was downright cramped.

"You can cope with it for the summer, can't you, girls?" Mom had asked the night before Katherine arrived. It was an excellent example of your basic parental rhetorical question.

To make room for Katherine, Mom bought used bunk beds at the Salvation Army. To make room for the bunks, we moved Joyce's bed into Shel's room down the hall. Joyce and Katherine slept in the bunk beds while I, the oldest, got to keep my bed.

As Joyce and Katherine slapped cards down over there in the window seat, I got the book I was currently reading, *Great Expectations,* and lay down on my bed. I looked up when Joyce started giggling.

"She just dropped all her cards," she told me. Turning back to Katherine, she said, "Lay them out again, butter fingers."

Going back to my book, I thought, Those two certainly get on well. It made sense, though. Katherine was right in the middle of us Reillys—she was two years older than Joyce and three years younger than Shel and me.

Meanwhile, she looked older than I did. And, as I'd just learned, you had to be unusually pretty to get away with that close-cropped hairstyle. If only I had big hazel eyes and glossy dark hair, I thought glumly. Okay, so I admitted it—I was kind of young- and gawky-looking even before I got scalped. But now that I was nearly bald, I looked like a brown-eyed, plucked *chicken.*

"That book must be pretty funny, Ab," Joyce said.

"Some parts," I answered, though I hadn't started reading yet.

"Katherine says she was nine the last time she visited us," Joyce said. "Is that right?"

I nodded. "I remember Shel and I had just turned twelve. Katherine and I were still tomboys then, in the—" I bit my lip to keep from saying, *in the old days when life was perfect.*

But it was true. In the old days, we were a very happy family. About the happiest family anyone ever heard of. For one thing, our parents were uncommonly happy together, and I knew it even as a little kid.

In the old days, we lived in a little village in upstate New York, where my parents published a weekly newspaper. They worked five-and-a-half days a week getting the paper out. I think not having them around much was why Shel, Joyce, and I have always been close.

Our parents were close; we three kids were close. It was perfect—the perfect past tense.

"What are you thinking about?"

I looked up to find Katherine studying me. "Nothing much," I answered. "Why?"

"Your face is very expressive, Abbey. One minute, you're smiling. The next, it's like a cloud passing over the sun."

"Expressive, huh?" I managed a laugh. "That's a first."

Joyce fixed me with serious brown eyes, asking, "You're not sad, are you, Ab?"

"Of course not. Now play cards, you two, and quit watching me."

But Katherine tilted her head, saying, "I don't care what anyone else thinks, I think your long hair was overpowering. Your face is really very interesting, Abbey."

"Really?" I grabbed a hand mirror off my bureau and stared at myself. After a moment, I sighed. "It looks like the same old small face with a ski-jump nose in the middle of it to me, brother. And I have a *lot* more freckles already. Just wait until I've spent a summer basking."

"Basking?" Joyce laughed. "I don't think you're going to spend much time lying around in the sun while baby-sitting three little kids, Ab."

"Short hair will be more comfortable in this hot weather," Katherine pointed out. "Please don't be angry at me, Abbey."

"I'm not," I said, avoiding her eyes. "You're probably right about short hair being more comfortable. Connecticut's much muggier than it was at home. . . ." My voice trailed off.

"Good thing Shel wasn't around to hear her say that," Joyce told Katherine as I bent my head over my book, pretending to read again.

Mom made us move after my father died. She chose Connecticut because Gram, my father's mother, lived in Greenwich. We were a little short on family. The only other relatives we had were Aunt Claudia and Katherine, and we certainly couldn't afford to move to Europe. So we rented a house in Norwalk, Connecticut.

It was July now. We had been here for eight months. Our rented house (which Shel referred to as "the little dump on the hill") seemed like home . . . almost. It was nothing like our old house. Our old house was special. It sat high on a hill overlooking a valley, and there was lots of space for all of us.

Now we lived in a small, brown-shingled Cape Cod that sat on a rise at the end of an unpaved road. I looked around the room, crammed with furniture, and sighed. Shel kept insisting that change is good, but . . .

"You're sighing," Katherine pointed out. "Please tell me what I can do to make it up to you, Abbey."

"You can quit watching me, for starters!"

"She doesn't mean it," Joyce told Katherine. "Abbey's the sweetest person in the world. I've noticed you do watch her a lot, though. How come?"

"Because I look up to her?" Katherine asked. Joyce nodded so seriously, I had to laugh a little. "What can I do to make it up to you, Abbey?"

"Katherine . . ."

"But you hate the way I cut it, and—"

"It's not that big a deal," I insisted, thinking, Just the end of a beautiful relationship between me and Rick Risteen. "Hair grows, remember?" I asked. "Hmm . . . I wonder how long it will be by the time school starts in September."

The door flew open. "It *might* cover your ears by then, dog face!" Sheldon yelled.

"Get out of our room!" Joyce and I screeched in unison. This time, *I* slammed the door in his vilely grinning face.

"Ab, look at her." Joyce nodded at Katherine, who held her sides, having silent hysterics.

Putting a hand on her arm, Joyce said, "You'll have to learn not to laugh at him, Katherine. It's the worst thing you can do."

"Why?" she asked.

"It encourages him," I explained.

"What's wrong with that? I'd love to have a brother like Shel; I'd just love it."

Joyce rolled her eyes. "She knows not whereof she speaks, Ab."

"You're telling me," I agreed as our cousin started laughing again.

Two

My best friend Mona Lisa Roche and I were considering majoring in business in college. After the success of R & R Service, a business we started last spring, we figured we must have some talent. We had so much work, we'd begun subcontracting jobs out to other people—namely, my brother and sister. Just last week, I had sent Shel out on a painting job and Joyce to a neighbor's to weed a garden.

One of the good things about being your own boss was that you could choose the jobs you wanted to do yourself. And when it came to something both Mona and I enjoyed, like taking care of Buster Grabinski, we shared.

Mona was so crazy about Buster that she'd helped me do the evening feeding every day this past week even though she did the morning feeding, too. Now, as I came over the rise in the road, I spotted her waiting for me.

She waved, calling, "What's with the cowboy hat, Ab?"

I didn't answer. I walked up to her and stopped. Then I took off the hat. She gasped.

"At least you're honest," I said, and started to put

the hat back on, but she stopped me.

Her blue-green eyes were round in her round face. "Abbey . . . it's absolutely *stunning*."

"*Stunning* pretty much hits the nail on the head, sports fan. *My* head, anyway. I hate it."

"Well, you're crazy. You look cute, Abbey."

"*Cute?*" I put the cowboy hat back on. "Let's go back to stunning."

She laughed as we started walking toward the Grabinskis' house.

A few minutes later, Mona leaned against Buster's stall, watching as I deposited a shovelful of his deposits into the wheelbarrow. "What kind of horse is Buster, anyway?" she asked.

"Mrs. Grabinski says he's a gray."

"But he's white, Ab."

"Yeah, but he's called a gray. He's also a mutt. Have you noticed how his head is too big for his body? And his little skinny eyebrows remind me of Packy Cowburn's."

She grinned. "Good thing Packy isn't around to hear you say that. I know what you mean, though. Have you heard from him since he went to Maine?"

"No." As I pushed the wheelbarrow around to the manure pile and dumped it, I said, "I'm plenty mad at him, too. Some friend *he* turned out to be."

"He's probably just playing hard-to-get. You know how much he likes you, Ab."

"And I like him . . . but only as a friend."

"Poor Packy." She sighed.

As I put the wheelbarrow away, I said, "You know, Mona, I've been thinking lately that maybe I value superficial things in people."

"What do you mean?" she asked.

"Well, maybe I care too much about appearances instead of what's inside."

She shrugged. "If you're worried about it, why don't you stop doing it, Abbey?"

I picked up the broom and began sweeping the cement floor. "You mean I can control being attracted to tall, dark, and handsome types?"

"Sure. Look what kind of person Don Champion turned out to be," she said.

"Don't remind me," I said.

Don Champion is this very good-looking boy who goes to Fitchett Academy, the private day school Gram sends Shel to. Mona was dating Don when I fell madly in love with him last spring. Fortunately, it didn't take me long to realize that he was disloyal and cowardly.

Now Mona asked, "Where's your cousin this afternoon?"

"She was designing doll clothes when I left. Mom gave Joyce her old Madame Alexander doll, and Joyce asked Katherine to make clothes for it. Did I tell you Katherine wants to be a 'wearable artist'?"

"No, but I'm impressed. Is that another name for a fashion designer?"

"Katherine says there's a difference," I answered. "Imagine knowing what you want to be when you're only thirteen, Mona. Sometimes it's hard being related to someone like Katherine." I met her eyes briefly before she turned away to close the back door of the barn.

"I can understand that," she said as I poured oats into Buster's bucket. "Listen to the thundering hooves," she added, grinning. A moment later, Buster came barreling through the paddock and into his stall. Mona went around to close the paddock gate while I climbed up into the loft to throw some hay down for Buster.

As we crossed the pasture a short time later, Mona said, "Look at it this way—if *we'd* grown up in Paris, we'd probably be supermature and gorgeous, too."

"It must be great, looking so together and grown-up and everything," I said as we climbed over the fence.

"Maybe not, Ab. Maybe there are drawbacks to it."

"Maybe," I said doubtfully as we started down the road. "Oh, well, at least we have good personalities, right, Mona?"

"Yep, and all the other girls like us!" she said, slapping me on the back, making me laugh. "I have to admit I was glad when I saw you were alone this afternoon, Ab. I haven't seen you alone since Katherine arrived last week."

"I know it. Why don't we do something together tomorrow night after we check Mrs. Winch's house, Mona? We could drive over to Cook's or something.

I know Mom will say Katherine's too young to go to a high school hangout, so it would be a perfect excuse to do something without her."

"Sounds like a good idea. Which reminds me, did I tell you what I had to go through to get my mother to let me take the house-sitting job, Abbey?" She rolled her luminous eyes and shook her head. "I had to *promise* that you and I would check the house together, that I'd never be there by myself. My mother's afraid I'll get kidnapped or something." She laughed.

"Honestly. You wonder when parents will quit treating us like children."

"You know it," she agreed. "I mean, what do they think will *happen* while we walk around a house checking the doors?"

"My mother was nervous about me house-sitting, too," I said. "She insisted that I write down the number of the police department and keep it by the phone in case something goes wrong over at the Winches'."

"What *could* go wrong?" she asked. "Well, I've decided that when I have children, I'm not going to be a worrywart like my mom. I'm going to show my kids that I trust them to use their heads."

"Speaking of children," I said as we reached the intersection of Perry Hill and Silverwood, "I start baby-sitting the Costello kids tomorrow. I told you about Rick Risteen being the lifeguard at their club, didn't I?"

She gave me a look. "Only about a hundred times, Abbey."

I laughed. "Sorry about that. He's just so good-looking."

"Yep," she said, flinging back her wavy, honey-colored hair. "Almost as good-looking as Don Champion, I bet."

"I'm doing it again, aren't I? Brother, I've got to get over this attraction to super-good-looking guys. I mean, how *shallow* can you get?"

She grinned. "Speaking of good-looking guys, who is your, uh, brother going out with this summer?"

"No one that I know of," I answered. "Why? You want me to put in a good word for you?"

"No. . . ." She lowered her eyes. "Shel knows where to find me. Let's face it, Abbey—your brother just isn't interested in me."

"He should be," I said, feeling bad for her. "You're a much nicer person than Crystal Glass," I added. Crystal is a girl in our class at school. She and Mona have been friends for years. Shel was madly in love with Crystal for a while. Crystal cheated during a track meet last spring, making me lose, but I took care of her in my own way. "I wish Shel would realize how great you are, Mona."

"Oh, well. . . ." She shrugged. "So, I'll pick you up after dinner tomorrow. We'll check the Winches' house around eight, then drive over to Cook's, see who's there."

"Great," I said. "See you then."

I had walked about half a mile before I noticed the purplish clouds gathering overhead. That was one of the differences between upstate New York and here. Thunderstorms were more frequent and spectacular here than they were at home—I mean, where we used to live.

Just the night before, Shel had lectured me about referring to the old house as home. "We've lived here eight months," he'd said. "Time for you to put the past behind you."

My response had been a giant Bronx cheer. I knew it was immature of me, but sometimes the only way to deal with Sheldon was to fight fire with fire, sports fans.

As the first raindrops hit, I grinned and broke into a run.

Three

I burst through the front door just ahead of the downpour, calling, "I'm home!"

No one heard me. The golden boy was upstairs, singing and strumming on his guitar like a maniac. He was singing "Blowin' in the Wind," a Bob Dylan song from the sixties. Sheldon was into the sixties these days.

Unfortunately, his singing voice resembled fifteen tomcats fighting over a fish head. Sticking my fingers in my ears, I headed for the kitchen.

"Whew!" I let the door swing shut behind me. "How do you stand it, Ma?" She stood in front of the open refrigerator, staring into space. "Ma?" I went over and tapped her on the shoulder.

"Oh, hi, dear," she said, coming back to earth. "Where have you been?"

"Mona and I have been taking care of Buster Grabinski for the past week, remember?" I asked patiently. You had to be patient with her these days. She'd been a little vague ever since she started going out with Kevin Macartney.

Not that I had anything against Mr. Macartney. He was nice enough.

He just wasn't Dad.

"Why are you looking at me like that?" my mother asked.

"Like what?"

"You're glaring at me," she said.

"Sorry." I leaned an elbow on her shoulder, adding, "Hey, Ma, you'd freak out if one of us kids kept the refrigerator door open that long. What are you looking for?"

"Chicken," she answered, reaching for the stack of packaged chicken breasts right there on the top shelf. "I'm trying a new recipe tonight."

"Really? What're we having?"

"*Suprêmes des volailles farcies aux épinards,*" she answered with a flourish.

I gave her a look. "You know French isn't my strong suit."

"Speaking of that, Abbey, why don't you take advantage of having your cousin here this summer and ask her to speak French to you so you can improve your accent and vocabulary?"

"And so I can develop a worse inferiority complex than I already have?" I asked sweetly.

"Oh, Abbey, you don't have any reason to feel inferior to anyone."

"That's what you think," I said, and whipped off my cowboy hat.

The only mother I had gasped and put a hand to her mouth. Finally, she managed, "How *cute!*"

"Thanks. Meanwhile, I was hoping to look gorgeous and alluring, like, well, like Katherine."

"Oh, Abbey . . ." She chuckled, shaking her head. "You and Katherine are completely different types, dear heart. Well, never mind. It will grow out."

"That's what I keep telling myself," I said. I pulled out a chair and sat down. "So, how about telling me in English what we're having for dinner?"

"Chicken breasts stuffed with spinach. I'm fixing it now because Kevin and I might go to a movie."

I was in the middle of miming "Kevin and I might go to a movie" when she turned to look at me. Giving her a giant fake smile, I said, fast, "Want some help?"

"You could skin and bone the chicken breasts for me."

"Skin and bone . . . ?" I got up and staggered around, making loud gagging noises. "Ma, would you please buy the already-boned chicken in the future? You *know* how I feel about raw chicken!"

"We're on a tight budget, Abbey. This chicken was on special." She opened a drawer and took out the rolling pin. "After you've skinned and boned it," she said, "you'll need this."

"Boy, oh, boy." I sighed, taking the rolling pin. "You offer to help in this house, and they reward you by giving you the most disgusting, despicable job they can—" The phone rang.

"I'll get it!" my mother cried, leaping to answer it. "Kevin!" she said like it was a surprise. "How *are* you?"

Meanwhile, this was probably the third time he'd called today, I thought, darkly. Brother, was I going to be glad when she quit seeing him and things got back to normal around here.

Keeping one eye on my mother, I picked up a chicken breast and shook it. Nothing happened. I shook it again. The skin remained securely attached. *Jesus, Mary, and Joseph,* you mean I'm going to have to *touch* raw flesh in order to skin it?

As my mother burst into your basic girlish peals at something old Kevin was saying, I closed my eyes, took a deep breath, and *ripped* the skin off the chicken.

Whew! I gasped, hanging on to the counter. I'd survived without throwing up. One down and seven to go.

"Excuse me, Kev," said Mom. "Abbey, what are you doing?"

"Breathing," I panted. "I sure hope this doesn't make me sick. I sure hope I don't vomit all over the *kitchen.* I sure hope—"

She turned her back on me. Into the phone, she said, "Don't even ask," and started laughing again. Taking another deep breath, I picked up a second chicken breast and *yanked* the skin off just as my mother said, "You're so nice to me, sweetheart."

The naked chicken slipped out of my hands and skidded across the counter. I couldn't have heard that right. Grabbing a package of chicken, I scuttled down the counter toward her.

Maybe she called him that out of habit, without thinking, I reasoned. Maybe if I hovered, made myself obvious, she'd realize what she'd done. If I breathed heavily while throwing the chicken around like this . . . she'd remember that she called Dad sweetheart.

How could she call anyone else that? I thought, fighting back tears.

That's when Mom turned and looked right at me, asking, "Could we go to the late show, sweetheart? That way, I'd have time to feed the kids first."

I was so upset that I skinned the rest of the chicken without further ado. Then I rinsed it under cold water and stacked it neatly on a plate. She was still on the phone.

Did I look like someone who *instinctively* knew how to bone chicken? I wondered.

"Oh, Kev, you're so funny!" my mother said, unnecessarily, as she burst into more merry peals.

I cleared my throat. "Excuse me, but I don't know how to . . . Mom?" Her tinkling laughing filled the room. "*Mom,* I said I don't know how to . . ."

She looked at me and stopped laughing. "I have to get off now, Kev. Yes, see you later, sweetheart." She hung up the phone and put her hands on her hips. "Honestly, Abbey, you'd think I could take a phone call without being interrupted."

I let my mouth hang open in righteous indignation, but it was lost on her. She was too busy getting a knife out of the drawer. Within seconds, it seemed, she'd boned the chicken. "There," she said, washing her hands. "Now all you have to do is pound it flat."

I picked up the rolling pin, asking, "Like this?" and gave the stack of chicken a tap.

"I wonder if it's too warm to wear slacks tonight," she said thoughtfully. "No, the theater will be air-conditioned. . . ."

"Or like this?" I gave the chicken a *whap*.

That got her attention. She narrowed her eyes, saying, "A little more gently, if you don't mind, Abernathy. I'm going to take a bubble bath." She only called me by my full name, which was her maiden name, when she was mad at me.

A few minutes later, Sheldon pounded down the stairs and blasted through the swinging door. "Jeez, dog face! What are you *doing* in here?"

"Just working out a few frustrations," I answered. "And don't call me dog face. I'm feeling a little sensitive about my face . . . now that it's the most prominent thing above my neck."

He laughed and slapped me on the back. "What's wrong, Ab?"

"She makes me want to barf, the way she talks to him," I muttered.

"Oh, for crying out loud. Are you bent out of shape over Mr. Mac again? Give it a rest, Abbey. There's nothing you can do about it. She *likes* the guy."

"I know it." I sighed and tossed the rolling pin into the sink.

29

"You know something?" He studied me. "I think I've gotten over the initial shock and I'm starting to like your hair that short. You look good, Ab. I mean it."

I narrowed my eyes, asking, "What do you want, Sheldon?"

He raised his blond eyebrows, as only he could, saying, "I'm serious! I'm really starting to like your new hairs."

"My new hairs, huh?" I laughed; I couldn't help it.

"Heck, you'd probably look good no matter how you wore your hairs." He gave me another brotherly slap on the back, adding, "Now, I want you to do me one favor—"

"I knew it! You've been insulting me since we came out of the womb. The only time you're nice to me is when you want something."

"All I want is for you to act as if you think Mr. Mac is okay, Abbey. I want you to . . . just get over being jealous, or whatever your problem is. For Mom's sake, Ab, if not for your own."

After a moment, I said, "I'll try, but I think maybe that's easier said than done. I mean, how do you get over resenting someone?"

He shrugged, giving me his best golden-boy smile. "Just do what *I* do, Ab."

"Boy, oh, boy." I sighed. "Here it comes—another lecture. What is it you do, O golden one?"

"I try to accept some things, Ab. Not that I always

succeed. But why make yourself miserable over things you can't control? Like who Mom dates, for instance. How would you like it if she made it obvious she disliked some guy you were crazy about?"

I opened my mouth to give him a snappy retort . . . but nothing occurred to me. "I wouldn't like it," I admitted. "It's just . . . she never has time to talk to me anymore. She's always racing around getting ready to see him."

"*Whine,*" Sheldon whined, making me laugh again.

"Well, she's always on the phone with him," I said.

"Yeah, and ever since Katherine came, you never have time to talk to me anymore."

I stared at him. "You mean you *care?*" I asked.

He shrugged, avoiding my eyes. "Everything's different with Katherine here. We'll get used to it, I figure. You have to make room, I guess, for new additions to the family, Ab." Then he patted my head.

"Quit that!" I yelled. "You know I hate that!"

"That's why I do it," he said, patting away. When I swung at him, he took off, chortling like a madman, just as Katherine and Joyce came through the back door.

"What's going on?" Joyce asked.

"Shel's harassing me, what else?" I answered. "He knows I can't stand to have my head touched!" Katherine started laughing.

"Come on up to our room and look at the designs Katherine did for my Madame Alexander, Abbey," my sister said. As we left the kitchen, she added, "Katherine's a wicked good designer; I mean it."

"I'm sure. Now, look," I said, "Shel's probably planning to ambush us at the top of the stairs or something. So be on your guard."

"Don't worry, Katherine," Joyce said, noticing her expression. "We'll protect you."

"How?" she asked. "He's bigger than we are."

"You've got long legs," Joyce said. "Use them like this." She aimed a few kicks at the dining room table as we passed.

"Not really." Katherine laughed. "I can't imagine kicking anyone, much less Shel."

"Well, you better learn," I told her, "because screaming at him—"

"Or slamming doors in his face," Joyce added.

"—has no effect most of the time," I said.

"Having a brother like Sheldon teaches you to fight back," Joyce explained.

As we started up the stairs, our cousin said, "You two are so lucky."

Four

"You're a good cook, Aunt Evelyn," Katherine said, as she put her fork down that night.

As Joyce and I got up to clear the table, Mom said, "Thank you, dear. Abbey helped—"

She was cut off by Sheldon saying in a loud voice, "Stop pinching me as you walk past my chair, Abbey!" I gave him a couple of head noogies and Joyce erupted into giggles.

"Honestly," said Mom. "I wonder what your cousin thinks of the way you three behave."

Meanwhile, Sheldon _had_ taken the hint and gotten off his duff to help Joyce and me.

"Let me help, too." Katherine started to get up.

Mom put out her hand, stopping her. "Oh, no, dear. You're a guest."

A funny expression crossed Katherine's face, but she smiled when Shel said, "She's family, Ma."

As Katherine followed us out to the kitchen, Mom said, "You kids can clean up without me, can't you? I want to put on some lipstick before Kevin gets here. Better vacuum under the table. . . . I see quite a few crumbs."

"Sure, Mom," said Shel. "You go ahead."

As I whipped the vacuum over the dining room rug in record time, I remembered the days when Mom was fairly relaxed about the house. The *minute* she started going out with Kevin Macartney, she became a neat freak. She started rushing around the minute she got home from work, cleaning up just in case Kevin dropped by.

In the old days, I thought as I put the vacuum away in the closet under the stairs, Mom didn't notice dust balls or a stray pair of underpants draped over a doorknob any more than we kids did. She changed when Mr. Macartney came into her life.

"Hey, Ab!" Sheldon called from the kitchen. "Quit moping around out there and get in here. It's your night to wash."

As I filled the sink with hot water, Katherine asked, "What can I do?"

Instantly Shel piped up, "Long as Abbey's washing and Joyce is drying, you can help me put away. What?" he asked, smiling innocently when Joyce and I glared at him.

The four of us worked in silence for a while. Suddenly, Joyce said, "Where's your father, Katherine? I never hear anything about him."

Shel dropped a plastic glass. "Uh, Joyce . . ."

"Better not ask personal questions, babycakes," I said.

"It's all right," Katherine said. She picked up the plastic glass and put it in the cupboard. "As far as I know, my father lives in New York."

"New York *City?*" I asked.

She nodded. "Claudia gave me his address before I came here."

"Well, that's great," I said. "You can visit him sometime this summer."

There was a pause. Then Shel asked, "Are you planning to visit him, Katherine?"

"I don't know . . . or rather, I haven't decided."

Joyce's eyes grew bigger and bigger as she stared first at Katherine, then at Shel and me. "But why?" she finally asked. "Why wouldn't you visit your own father?"

"Because I've never met him, never spoken to him, *chérie.*"

"How can that be?" my little sister asked.

"My parents divorced when I was a baby," Katherine explained. "Claudia and I stayed in Paris; my father came back to the United States. I've never had any contact with him." She lifted her shoulders in a small shrug as if to say, It's as simple as that.

"That's awful," I said, after a moment. "I'm sorry for you, Katherine."

"Me, too," Shel said. "I always wondered about your old man. . . . Mom and Dad were so close-mouthed about him."

She glanced at the three of us. "I've thought about contacting him . . . if I can muster the courage."

Putting a hand on her shoulder, Shel said, "We'd be glad to go with you, if it'd help. All four of us could go some weekend. We three could explore while you spend some time with your father, Katherine. Then we'd meet you and go home together. How's that sound?" He looked at Joyce and me.

"That's the best idea you've had in months, Sheldon," said Joyce. I laughed at her tone, and at the same time I felt a sudden rush of affection for my twin. Sometimes, Sheldon could be the kindest, most considerate person in the world.

Katherine smiled at him. "Thank you, Shel. I might take you up on it. I'd be too afraid to go by myself. . . ."

"I really don't understand this," Joyce said, sighing.

Shel shook his head. "She's never *met* the guy. Imagine that."

"I can't," I said. "I just can't."

"Now you all look sad," Katherine pointed out. "I'm sure I'll feel braver by the end of the summer. Living with you three will probably toughen me up."

As if on cue, Shel faked a punch to her arm, saying, "We'll do what we can—right, Ab?" Katherine started laughing, which naturally made him act even more obnoxious. The next thing I knew, he'd abandoned the fake punches and was landing the genuine variety—on me.

"Cut it out!" I hollered. "*Why* do you always have to start horsing around? Mom!" I yelled, ducking. By this time, I was also laughing. "*Quit it!*"

"Quit it!" he mimicked, dancing around me. So I waited until he was directly in front of me. Then I gave him a push.

Like all of us Reillys, Shel was the lithe, wiry type. I didn't push him *that* hard, but he flew backward, landing on our old kitchen table—which split in two.

"Ab!" Joyce gasped.

"Are you hurt?" Katherine asked, helping Shel up.

"I don't think so, but this table sure is. Nice play, Shakespeare," he added, glaring at me. "Now you've really done it, man."

"*I've* done it? *You've* got a nerve!" I sputtered.

Behind me, my mother said, "I can't believe it. At your ages you're *still* destroying the furniture. Who is responsible for this?"

"Shel started it, Mom," said Joyce.

The golden boy hung his head. "We were just messing around, Mom, and . . . Abbey pushed me."

I gasped, preparing to scratch his eyes out, at least.

But Mom closed hers, saying, "I can't deal with this now. Abernathy, you and Sheldon will pay to have the table fixed." She opened her eyes and looked only at me, adding, "You should be ashamed of yourselves. I apologize for my children's babyish behavior, Katherine. Kevin is due here any minute. I don't want to hear another peep out of any of you." She turned and left the room.

"I'll get you for this, you toad!" I shook my fist at my twin.

"It *was* my fault," he admitted.

I stared at him for a second. Then I hit my head, saying, "I couldn't have heard that correctly." Joyce burst into giggles.

Putting his arm around me, Shel said, "I apologize, Ab. From now on, it's going to be nothing but kisses and hugs for you."

With that, he puckered up and pasted a wet one on my cheek, and I screamed. Brother, did I scream.

"Jeez!" he said, letting me go. "Deafen me for *life,* why don'tcha?"

Joyce and Katherine were hanging on to each other, they were laughing so hard. "Sh!" I hissed as the doorbell rang.

A moment later, Mom called, "I'm going, children. See you in the morning."

Five

Joyce and I let Katherine use the bathroom first. By the time we'd changed into our pj's, brushed our teeth, and gotten back to our room, she was already in bed.

"You're not going to sleep, are you?" Joyce asked her. "It's only nine o'clock."

"I usually go to bed early when I don't have a date, *chérie*."

Joyce shot me a meaningful look, saying, "I'll bet you have a lot of them, don't you, Katherine?"

"Actually, yes, I do."

"Abbey's only had a couple, even though she's older'n you," good old Joyce informed her. "She had some boys calling her in the spring, but since school ended a few weeks ago, her social life's sort of pooped out."

"Joyce, if you don't mind—," I began.

"What were you putting on your face when we walked in, Katherine?" Joyce asked, getting into bed.

"A cream to keep my skin from wrinkling. You're never too young to start taking care of yourself, you know," Katherine replied.

Suddenly, I was aware of Joyce peering at me from the lower bunk. "Maybe you should start using face cream, too, Ab. Gosh, you *are* getting freckly!"

I gave her a long look before saying, "Thank you so much." Katherine broke up. "Why don't you read for a while, Joyce . . . like Katherine." Katherine who seems to be your newest heroine, I thought.

"Hey, Ab, I just remembered something. Did I tell you what Kevin said about you and Katherine when he took Mom and me out to lunch last Saturday?"

"No." I bent my head, pretending to read.

"What did he say?" Katherine finally asked.

"He said you and Abbey were totally different types. You're polished and Abbey's more the outdoor type."

I looked up from *Great Expectations*. "Gee, thanks. That makes me feel glorious."

Katherine started laughing again. "Oh, Abbey, you're so funny."

"He meant it in a good way," Joyce told me. "He meant that Katherine's beautiful, but you're—"

Katherine buried her face in the pillow as I cried, "This gets better and better!"

"Kev said you were *fresh*-looking, Ab. He also said he only had to look at you to know you were bright, too."

"He did? Kevin said—?" I caught myself and shrugged. "So?"

"He's a nice man, Abbey. I wish you liked him."

"I like him fine, Joyce. Now, let's everyone read her book."

A moment later, Joyce asked, "What're you reading?" I looked up to answer—

"Poetry," Katherine said. "You'll probably think it's stupid that I like it, but it's calming . . . especially when I'm nervous or upset."

"About your father," Joyce said, somberly. "I don't blame you for being upset about him, Katherine."

"Speaking of all of that . . ." I closed my book. "I wanted to ask about your mom, Katherine. I know she's looking for a job, but what if she doesn't find one by the end of the . . . ?" My voice trailed off as I noticed the expression on her face, the way she plucked at her lacy, pale-blue nightgown. "That's a really pretty nightgown," I blurted, changing the subject. "Did you get that from your mom?"

I figured it had to be an old one of Aunt Claudia's because it was low-cut and sexy. But Katherine shook her head, answering, "It was a gift from a friend of my mother's."

I stared at her, wondering what kind of friends Aunt Claudia had. "Oh," I said, pulling myself together, "well, your mother's friend has good taste."

"I suppose that's one thing that can be said for André," she said in an odd tone.

"You mean a *man* gave you that?"

She almost smiled, saying, "You look scandalized, Abbey. André was a choirboy compared to my mother's latest. . . . Let's not talk about this now," she added, pointing at the lower bunk.

Meanwhile, Joyce's ears were practically pricking up through her wispy hair. As she opened her mouth to ask about Aunt Claudia's latest, I said quickly, "If you like poetry, you've come to the right house, Katherine. My father loved it, you know."

"Did he?" she asked, sounding wistful.

I nodded. "He used to make me and Shel memorize it when we were little. He made a kind of competition out of who could memorize a poem the fastest."

"You're so lucky," she said. "You don't realize."

I chuckled. "Shel and I didn't think we were lucky at the time."

"I remember Shel shouting at Dad one time that he wouldn't do it," said Joyce.

"Not shouting exactly," I contradicted.

"He did, too," she insisted. "Shel and Dad argued a lot," she told Katherine. "Even Mom says they had a stormy relationship. Abbey likes to believe everything was perfect, but—"

"I'm glad Dad made us memorize poems," I interrupted, "because now when I remember them, it reminds me of him."

"Let me recite our favorite, Ab," Joyce said, and did.

"An' all us other children, when the supper things is done,
We set around the kitchen fire an' has the mostest fun

A-list'nin' to the witch-tales 'at Annie tells about,
An' the Gobble-uns 'at gits you ef you don't watch out!"

"Good job," I told my sister.

"What is that from?" Katherine asked.

"'Little Orphan Annie,' by James Whitcomb Riley," Joyce answered. "No relation to us."

"We all loved that one," I said. "I remember the first time Dad read it to Shel and me. It was during a flood we had in upstate New York. . . . This was years ago, when Joyce was just a baby. Anyway, we lost electricity for two days, so Dad kept a fire going in the fireplace all the time. We cooked over it, and at night we'd sit by the fire and Dad would read poetry. I remember being absolutely enthralled the first time I heard 'Little Orphan Annie.' It became a family tradition—Dad or Mom reading it aloud."

Katherine hugged her knees to her chest. "I'd give anything to have memories like that."

I nodded, thinking, But memories aren't enough. "Hey," I whispered, "Joyce is asleep. Now you can tell me about your mother's latest friend, Katherine."

She moved restlessly in the bunk. Finally, she whispered, "She started seeing him immediately after she broke it off with André."

"After giving you that nightgown, I would think your mother would break it off," I interrupted.

"The nightgown had nothing to do with it. My mother got tired of André, and one night he told her I was too innocent for my age."

43

"That's outrageous!" I squeaked. "What kind of dirty old man is this guy?"

"You just described him perfectly, Abbey."

"I'll bet your mother was furious. No wonder she broke up with him. Wait a minute—don't tell me you're a kindred spirit, Katherine." I grinned at her.

She looked puzzled. "What do you mean?"

"Don't kid me," I said. "You must eavesdrop the way I do."

"I don't have to eavesdrop, Abbey," she said, matter-of-factly. "Claudia tells me everything. She considers me her equal."

"But you're only thirteen. How can you be your mother's equal at thirteen?"

"Claudia says the only difference between children and adults is experience," she replied earnestly. "I've been raised as my mother's equal."

"Hasn't that been hard on you?" I asked.

"Don't sound so shocked," she said after a moment. "Claudia's a good mother. Really, she is. She treats me like an adult."

She looked unhappy again, so I decided to change the subject. "Well, it's good your mother's not dating André anymore, I guess," I said.

She made a face. "Yes. *Now* she's living with the count. . . ." She bit her lip, adding, "I wasn't supposed to tell. Promise me you won't tell Aunt Evelyn what I just said."

"Mom wouldn't care, Katherine. Don't get upset."

"You've got to *promise* me, Abbey."

"Take it easy," I whispered. "I promise, but I don't understand."

It was like a shade being pulled down. All expression left her face. "He's a bad man. I'll tell you how I know that sometime. . . . I'm too tired now. Let's go to sleep."

Long after I could tell my cousin was asleep, I lay there, staring into the darkness, wondering what it would be like if my mother considered me her equal . . . not to mention if she decided to live with a bad man.

Six

The first thing I thought of the next morning was that today I would see Rick Risteen. I was full of joie de vivre, not to mention beans . . . until I looked at myself in the bathroom mirror and saw my hair. Or rather, the lack of it. I groaned and put my head in my hands just as someone knocked on the door.

"Come in," I said into my hands.

The door opened. "I thought you might like to borrow this," my little sister said.

I raised my head. She held out her new leopard-print suede cap. "Joyce, you wonderful person, thanks a lot." I took the cap and put it on, pulling it low over my eyes.

"You look wicked good in that hat, Ab."

"Thanks." I grinned at myself in the mirror, muttering, "Rick Risteen, here I come."

"Who's Rick Risteen?"

"The superhandsome brother of a girl I know at school. He works at the Costellos' club. I met him at school in June when he picked his sister Janet up after a Short Story Committee meeting. You should see him, Joyce. He's wonderful—tall, dark, handsome, *and* a college man."

"But that stuff doesn't make someone wonderful."

I laughed. "What *more* do you want?"

She fixed me with her big brown eyes and said, "I never told you about the bad experience I had with Jiggy Graham last year, did I?"

"No," I said, surprised. "Isn't Jiggy Graham the kid you went to that dance at school with?"

She nodded. "The square dance. I'll never forget it. I guess it had to happen though. . . . At least it taught me a good lesson."

I sat down on the edge of the bathtub, saying, "Tell me about it, Joyce."

She sat down beside me and took a deep breath. "Well, Jiggy Graham was the cutest boy in fifth grade, so naturally I was happy when he asked me, the new girl, to go to the square dance. Jiggy is the type who's wicked cute and knows it, Ab, if you know what I mean."

"Of course I know what you mean. I'm your big sister, aren't I?" I stroked her wispy hair and remembered the snub-nosed little girl who used to crawl into my bed during thunderstorms, who came to me whenever she needed help or advice. "Oh, Joyce . . . you seem so grown-up. How did it happen?"

She shrugged. "I keep having birthdays?"

I grinned, saying, "Okay, wise guy; so tell me about your bad experience with Jiggy Graham."

"My first date was a big disappointment, Abbey. Jiggy's the kind of boy all the girls like, the kind who carries a comb around in his back pocket. . . ."

"So he can whip it out at a moment's notice to comb his hair in public?" I asked. She nodded. "I *hate* boys like that."

"You and me both, Ab. Anyway, we got to the square dance and the first thing Jiggy has to do is go to the boys' room to—guess what?"

"Do what people usually do in boys' rooms?"

She giggled. "No; Jiggy went to the boys' room to check out his hair! Not only that, he was a wicked *nerd* on the dance floor. I think he was so worried about how he looked that he didn't listen to the caller's instructions. Our teacher, Miss Festa, gave us a lesson before the music started, but I don't think Jiggy heard a word. I can hardly stand thinking about it. . . ." She shuddered.

"You can't leave me hanging," I said. "What happened?"

"First, we crashed into Libby Beardsell and Johnnie Wycoff. Libby is only the most popular girl in school, Ab. She fell down, skinned her knee, and burst into tears. She's hated my guts ever since, too.

"Anyway, after they sent her to the nurse's office, they started the music again so Jiggy could do the next dorky thing, which was to let go of me in the middle of a 'swing your partner.' We were moving so fast, I almost flew off into outer space. It wasn't funny," she added when I started laughing. "I could've died, Ab—seriously."

"I'm sorry," I said. "I can understand how embarrassed you were, but Joyce, it *is* funny."

She poked out her little lower lip. "Katherine didn't think so."

I quit laughing. "You told Katherine about this before you told your big *sister*?"

"Don't take it personally, Ab. It's just . . . Katherine treats me like I'm her age, you know? We *are* closer in age than you and I are. Plus, I was afraid to tell you how upset I was. . . . Jiggy said he'd never ask me to another dance."

"What a nerve," I said. "Who'd want to go with a *bozo* like him anyway?"

"Hmm." She frowned. "That's a good point, Ab. Anyway, I learned my lesson. Jiggy is cute, but it doesn't make up for his being a jerk."

"Well, I'm sure Rick Risteen's not like Jiggy Graham," I said confidently.

She shrugged. "If he does turn out to be like Jiggy, don't be too disappointed, Ab. Katherine says we have to kiss a lot of toads before we find our prince."

I nodded, but I thought, Katherine again.

This, I told myself a few hours later as I turned the fire-engine-red convertible up Country Club Drive, is a dream come true. When Mrs. Costello hired me, she said I'd be driving the kids to their club every day. But she never mentioned I'd be driving her new convertible.

"Here we are!" I announced as I parked the car. "Ready for a day of sunshine and fun, kids?"

"Yay!" they yelled, bouncing up and down in their car seats. The Costello kids were like stair steps: Cathy was four, Cora was three, and little Calvin was two. All three were absolutely angelic-looking, with dark hair and big blue eyes. I was looking forward to getting to know them. Whenever I baby-sat for them in the past, they were already in bed by the time I arrived.

It beat me why Mrs. Costello seemed so nervous, I thought as I got everyone out of their car seats. Before the kids and I left that morning, she gave me strict instructions to keep Calvin on a leash at all times. And when he was in the pool area, he had to wear a life jacket.

After snapping Cal's leash on, I tucked the beach towels under my arms and slung the lunch cooler around my neck. "Okay, kids," I said, "we're ready! You girls hold hands, and Cathy, you hold my free hand, okay? Now, we'll all cross the parking lot together. Don't forget to look both ways!"

We started off. So far, so good, I thought. I had everything under control . . . until Calvin spotted a couple of golfers zipping past in a golf cart.

"Me!" he yelled, and took off—sort of. I had wound the leash around my wrist twice.

"Hey!" I yelped. "My *arm*." Calvin stopped short and fell down just as I dropped all the towels.

"This way!" Cathy and Cora cried, pulling in the opposite direction. My hat fell off and the cooler swung around, hitting Cathy in the head. She started crying, which set off Cora, and, finally, Calvin.

It took me a while, but I finally got everyone calmed down, picked up all our gear, jammed Joyce's spotted hat back onto my head, and instructed everyone to move in the same direction at all times. Taking a deep breath, I led my little band up the steps to the pool area.

Everything was copacetic as we passed the lifeguard stand, where Rick Risteen sat looking like a bronzed god. I gave him one of my best model-type smiles . . . and got no reaction.

Hmm, I thought, smile fading. Maybe he didn't see me. He was surrounded by girls, after all. Of course, it could be he didn't recognize me in Joyce's hat. That was it, I thought, brightening up again. I'd just have to reintroduce myself to him sometime today.

"Now, kids," I said as we passed the snack bar, "remember that your mom wants us to stay in the baby-pool area at all times. No, Calvin, not that way, honey . . . this way, sweetheart." I reeled him in as he tried to make a break for the snack bar. "How about if I carry you? Doesn't that sound like fun?" I asked in that falsely cheerful voice that adults use on small children.

"No," he said, and began crying as I scooped him up with my free arm. Meanwhile, scooping up a solidly built two-year-old is no mean feat when you're loaded down like a packhorse.

"Girls, not so fast," I said as they pulled me

toward the fenced-in baby pool. Suddenly, Cathy let go of my hand and she and her little sister took off. "Come back here!" I yelled.

Thweet! Thweet! "No running in the pool area!" someone hollered. Thweet! Thweet!

Just as Calvin and I caught up to Cora and Cathy, I looked over my shoulder and saw Rick Risteen striding toward us. "Hi!" I greeted him.

Spitting the whistle out of his mouth, he snapped, "No running allowed in the pool area. Next time, I'll have to throw you out."

"Did you hear that, kids?" I asked as gently as I could. The girls nodded, looking stricken. "They won't do it again," I told Rick.

He squinted and pushed his pith helmet up off his forehead, asking, "Do I know you?"

"Yes, well, kind of. I'm a friend of your sister, Janet's. We met in June at my school?" I smiled hopefully.

"Uh, sure," he said, obviously in the dark. "What's your name again?"

"Abbey Reilly." Taking Cora's hand and shifting Calvin up higher on my hip, I added, "Well, we'll *walk* to the baby pool now, right kids?" I smiled at them. "Nice seeing you again, Rick."

As we walked away, he called, "Just make sure you keep those little rug rats under control."

Cathy scowled, saying, "We're not rats."

"Of course you aren't," I said, opening the gate to the baby pool. "It's just an expression."

"He won't throw us out, will he, Abbey?" Cora asked.

"No, don't worry, honey. Just remember not to run, okay?"

"I don't *like* him," Cathy said loudly.

"How about we spread our towels out by that chair over there," I said quickly. The girls headed in the direction I pointed.

A few minutes later, I sat on the side of the pool, watching the kids splash around. I glanced at the lifeguard stand—just as a voluptuous blond in a yellow bikini handed Rick a Coke.

Suddenly I felt a clammy hand on my knee. "That girl's pretty, isn't she?" Cathy asked in ringing tones. I turned a fetching shade of purple as Rick and his friend looked over at us.

"She certainly is," I whispered, pulling my cap down as far as I could. "Let me see how you swim, Cathy!" She jumped feetfirst into the pool, dousing me and a mother standing nearby.

Obviously, this was not going to be a summer to remember, I thought late that afternoon as the kids and I straggled past the lifeguard stand (vacant, now). They had begged me to let them stay until the baby pool closed. I'd agreed, hoping that Rick might wander over to talk to me if I was the only girl left. It hadn't happened.

I had Cal under one arm and most of our stuff under the other. The girls brought up the rear, trailing beach towels.

As we passed the ladies' room, the door opened, and the blond I'd seen talking to Rick earlier came out. I stopped so fast, Cathy and Cora nearly bumped into me.

In a sweet, lilting voice, she said, "I saw you talking to Rick."

I nodded. "His sister goes to school with me. . . ." My voice trailed off.

She was looking me up and down. "Nice hat," she remarked.

"Thanks. I just got my hair cut and I hate it. Well, guess the kids and I had better get going. Nice talking to you."

As I walked away, she called after me in that same pleasant voice, "You don't have a chance with him, you know."

"Ab-bey, come on!" Cathy shouted. She and Cora waited at the top of the steps.

"I'll be right there," I answered, glad for a reason to hurry.

"Were we bad today?" Cathy asked, slipping her hand into mine as we crossed the parking lot toward the car.

"Not at all. Why do you ask, honey?"

"You look mad."

"I'm not . . . not at you." I wiped the frown off my face and smiled at her.

As we reached Mrs. Costello's red convertible, someone called my name. I looked around to see Rick Risteen heading toward me. "Got a minute?" he asked.

"Sure. Just let me get the kids into their car seats." That done, I turned to him. "Hi," I said for the second time that day.

"Hi." He grinned. His teeth were very white in his tanned face. "I wanted to explain about Melissa."

"Melissa?"

"My . . . girlfriend." He shrugged. "Actually, she's an ex, but she won't accept it. Anyway, I overheard what she said to you just now and wanted to explain that she's still carrying a torch, but I could care less." He smiled.

"Oh," I said, for lack of anything better.

"You know, I didn't remember you this morning, Abbey. Then I realized it's your hair. You used to have long hair."

"I got it cut."

"No," he said. "Is that why it's so short?" I had to laugh. He did, too. His eyes crinkled at the corners when he did. "It's cute," he said.

Pulling the leopard-print cap down, I muttered, "Thanks."

"You know who you remind me of with your hair that short, Abbey?"

"Who?"

"Peter Pan! You look just like Peter Pan!"

"Peter Pan?" I repeated weakly. How many sixteen-year-old girls want to hear they look like Peter Pan? "Maybe I ought to invest in a wig."

He laughed uproariously. "You've got a great sense of humor, you know that? Well, I told Melissa I'd give her a ride home. I hope we get to know each other this summer, Abbey. How long are you taking care of the rug rats?"

"Until the end of the summer."

"Great!" He put a hand on my shoulder and looked deep into my eyes, adding, "Then we'll have plenty of opportunity to talk. Looking forward to seeing you tomorrow."

"What about Melissa?" I blurted.

"What about her?" he asked, and winked. "Life is short. Right?"

"Right," I said uncertainly. "Well, see you tomorrow."

"You bet!" He gave me a dazzling smile as I got into the car.

As I drove out of the parking lot, Cathy muttered, "We are not rats."

Seven

"How'd it go with Rick Risteen?" Joyce asked as soon as I walked into the house.

"Great . . . except he thinks I look like Peter Pan."

She laughed. "Peter Pan's cute, Ab."

"Yeah; he's also a *boy*. Come out to the kitchen with me while I raid the fridge. I'm starving to death."

"There's nothing to eat except fruit," she said. "I already checked."

"You're right," I said a moment later. "Brother, I wish Mom'd buy some *food* once in a while."

"She and Kevin are watching their weight," Joyce said.

I sniffed and sat down at the card table. (Mr. Macartney had picked up the broken kitchen table before work that morning. He *claimed* he could fix it.) "Rick says he wants to get to know me this summer," I told my sister. "That's one thing about a summer job. It's an excellent way to meet new and exciting people."

"That's exactly what I've been thinking," Katherine said, walking into the room.

"Hi," I greeted her. "Where have you been?"

She sat down on the stool by the phone and fanned herself. "I walked down to the post office to mail a letter to Claudia."

"That's quite a walk," I said. "Why didn't you just put the letter in the mailbox or wait until Mom came home with the car? Shel or I would've driven you down."

"Oh, I didn't have anything better to do. I was also hoping"—she lowered her hazel eyes—"to meet some girls my age in the neighborhood."

I stared at her. Girls like Katherine didn't get lonely, did they? "I guess we've all been pretty busy lately," I said. "Have we been ignoring you, Katherine?"

"No; I just wish I had something to do. I think it would make me feel more"—she dropped her eyes again—"like part of the family. Claudia gave me money, but I feel odd, not working like you and Shel do. Even Joyce earns her own money. If you get something you think I could do, would you hire me, Abbey?"

"Well, sure," I said. "What do you have experience with? Done any baby-sitting?"

"No."

"How about weeding?" Joyce asked. "Abbey's got a couple of people who always need that done."

"I'm sure I could learn," our cousin said. "It isn't difficult, is it?" Joyce and I looked at her hands, lying in her lap. They were lily-white and perfectly manicured. There wasn't so much as a chip in her bright-red nail polish.

Raising her eyes to mine, Joyce said, "I don't think she's the weeding type, Ab."

"Maybe I could take care of the Costello children once in a while," Katherine suggested. "If you had something else to do, Abbey."

I looked at her. She was so pretty with that sleek, dark hair and those big hazel eyes in her small, fine-boned face. . . . The Costello kids would run circles around her. Heck, they'd make *mincemeat* out of her.

"I'm willing to try anything," she added.

"Maybe something will come up next week," I hedged.

"Katherine and I were talking earlier," Joyce said, "and she was telling me about the last place she lived in France. Tell her about it, Katherine. About all the maids and everything."

The bright expression left my cousin's face as she said, "The Bouquets had a chauffeur and a cook—"

"And *two* maids." Joyce held two fingers in front of my face, making me laugh. "Imagine living like that!"

I looked around the kitchen. The card table was rickety and too small for the room, the linoleum was coming up in a couple of places, and you could barely see the front of the refrigerator, what with all of the notes and newspaper clippings and whatnot stuck on it.

Looking back at my cousin, I said, "Living here must freak you out."

She grinned. "Not at all. It's charming. I think I'll take a shower now. *À bientôt, mes cousines.*"

As soon as she left the room, Joyce gave me a piercing look. "You don't really think she *meant* that, do you, Ab?"

"That's what she said. . . . I'm not sure what she meant."

"Oops!" Joyce covered her mouth. "Speaking of people not meaning what they say—Mona Lisa Roche called and told me to tell you she'd kill you if you didn't call her the minute you walked in the door, Ab."

As I got up to call Mona back, I remembered saying that I wouldn't let Katherine tag along tonight. "Mona and I made plans to go out tonight, Joyce, but you'll be home, won't you?"

She shook her head. "Andrea Pratt asked me to come over to watch a movie with her on their new VCR and spend the night. Why?"

I held up a finger as Mona answered the phone. "Hi, sports fan," I said.

"Hi! Just wanted to remind you we're going out—just the two of us, right, after we check the Winches' house?"

"We're all set," I said. "I feel funny about it though. . . . Katherine's probably going to be the only one home tonight."

"Oh," she said. "Well, maybe we should take her with us."

"But she's not a little kid," I said. "I'll talk to her, sound her out." But when I hung up a short time later, I frowned.

"What?" my sister asked.

"Well, I'm busy tonight, Shel's got his class at Norwalk Community College, and you know Mom will probably go out with Kevin; so who's going to stay with Katherine?"

"She's used to being alone," Joyce said. "You know what she told me? She says she's been making all her own decisions for years."

"Really?"

She nodded. "Wouldn't that be great? Running your own life, not having to ask permission from your parents?"

"I guess so," I said. "Brother, no wonder Katherine's not like most thirteen-year-olds. Oh, well, maybe we'll all be home tomorrow night, so we can keep her company then."

My sister laughed. "Maybe we shouldn't do her any favors, Ab!"

Eight

"Remind me to bring a flashlight along tomorrow night," Mona said, clutching my shirttail as we rounded the side of Mrs. Winch's garage. "I thought I'd outgrown my fear of the dark, but I guess not."

"We're almost done," I said. "We checked the front door and the porch. Now all we have to do is check the back door. Don't be surprised if you see a light. Mrs. Winch said she'd leave the dining room light on."

"Yep, there's the light," Mona said a few seconds later. As I checked the back door, she headed for the lighted window. "*Ohmygod!* Abbey!"

"What's wrong?"

"There's an intruder in the Winches' house!"

"Now, Mona," I said, walking toward the bush she cowered behind, "are you sure? Where's this intruder?"

"There!" she gasped, and yanked me to the ground. *"Did you see him, Ab?"*

"How could I? You never gave me the chance."

"He's standing in front of the sideboard! That's probably where they keep their silver! Oh, Lord, what're we going to *do?*"

"First, calm down." I got to my knees and slowly raised myself until—"Holy To*l*edo!" I hit the dirt. "There *is* someone in there!"

"What should we do?" she quavered.

"Get the heck out of here! *Come on!*" We crawled at top speed around to the side of the house. "I think he was carrying a gun!" I whispered as we got to our feet.

"Well, don't just stand there!" she cried. *"Run!"* We sprinted for the car.

"Brother," I panted, locking all the doors as Mona tried to get her mother's car started. "I never thought I'd be glad for all those hours running track, but I am tonight. I've never seen *you* move so fast, Mona!"

She didn't answer; she was too busy grinding the gears. Finally, she got the car into first and we went roaring down the Winches' driveway to Silverwood Road.

"Why are you turning toward my house?" I asked. "Yours is closer."

"No way I can let my mom know about this, Abbey! She'd never let me out of her sight again!" She was hunched over the steering wheel, driving as if the hounds of hell were after us.

After checking over my shoulder, I said, "Slow down, Mona. No one's chasing us."

She eased up on the gas. "I have never been so scared in my life, Abbey. You better call the police as soon as we get to your house."

"Uh-oh," I said as she turned into my driveway.
"What?"

"Mr. and Mrs. Winch have a grown son. It just occurred to me—what if that guy was their son? Or what if it's a neighbor, someone who's supposed to be there? It doesn't make sense that a burglar would be standing in a lighted room, does it? Wouldn't he turn off the light if he was stealing the family silver?"

She pulled up at the foot of the steps and switched off the ignition. "You have a point, Ab. Did Mrs. Winch say she was going to leave the key with anyone?"

"No," I said as we got out of the car. "But it might've slipped her mind. I'm trying to think what to do to avoid making fools of ourselves. R & R has to protect its reputation."

"I just thought of something," Mona cried, following me up the steps. "We can ask your brother what we should do, Ab!"

"No, we can't. He's taking a course at the community college this summer. He's in class tonight."

Her face fell. "Oh."

"Besides that, we don't need my brother to tell us what to do, Mona. We can think for ourselves, can't we?"

"I guess," she answered as we went into the house. "But it'd be a lot more fun to ask Shel for help."

"This is no time for jokes, Mona."

"Sorry, Ab. What should we do about this?"

I was about to admit I didn't know when Katherine appeared at the top of the stairs. "Hello," she said. She looked really happy to see us.

"Hi, Katherine," Mona said. "I love your miniskirt. Did you get that in Paris?"

"Yes," Katherine answered as she came down the stairs. "You can borrow it if you'd like, Mona."

Mona chuckled. "Thanks, but I'm about fifteen sizes bigger than you are."

"Excuse me, fashion fans," I interrupted. "We have a problem here—a *serious* problem."

Mona bit her lip. "We sure do," she said. Then she told my cousin about the intruder in the Winches' dining room. "Abbey says maybe the guy's supposed to be there," she explained, "so we're trying to decide if we should call the police. It could be pretty embarrassing if the person's not a burglar, you know?"

Katherine nodded, looking thoughtful. "Why don't you call over there first?" she suggested. "If he answers the phone, you know it's all right. If he doesn't"—she shrugged—"it's a burglar."

Mona looked at her for a moment before turning to me, saying, "She's young, but wise beyond her years, Ab." I was already headed for the phone.

A short time later, I hung up. "Well, there's no answer. I guess we better call the police."

"Here's the number." Mona handed me the slip of paper Mom had insisted I write emergency numbers on.

After hanging up for a second time, I said, "The police will be there within ten minutes. They want us to meet them."

"We'd better get going," Mona said. "Thanks for your help, Katherine."

"Yeah, thanks a lot. And whatever you do, don't mention this to Mom," I told her.

"I won't, Abbey."

I started to leave the kitchen, then hesitated. My cousin stood there with her head lowered, playing with the telephone cord.

"Abbey?" Mona called from the hall. Her voice sounded hollow in the silent house.

"You want to come with us, Katherine?" I asked. She looked up and nodded. "Well, come on then!"

The three of us were hurrying down the front steps, when who should come peeling down the driveway.

"It's Shel!" Mona cried.

"I don't know why you sound so *relieved*," I complained. "We certainly have everything under control."

As if I hadn't spoken, she rushed over to Sheldon as he got out of the car. "Am I glad to see you!" she said. "Abbey and I need help!"

That's how Sheldon ended up in the passenger seat while Katherine and I shared the back of Mona's mother's Honda. Mona explained the situation to my twin as she drove back over to the Winches'.

As she turned into the driveway, Shel ordered,

"Douse the headlights." Mona did. "Slow down," he commanded. The next thing I knew, we were creeping up the driveway at one mile an hour. "Turn off here." She immediately did so.

Fortunately, before my twin could give any more orders, a pair of headlights turned into the driveway . . . followed by another pair . . . and another . . . and another.

A total of five patrol cars showed up. The police told us to stay put while they checked the house. They left the four of us huddled there in the dark.

I had to admit, it was spooky, especially when a dog began howling in the distance. That was when I realized Mona and Katherine were edging closer and closer to Sheldon. I looked around. It was pitch black. A thick hedge kept out any light from neighboring houses. I grabbed my brother's arm.

Just then a flashlight beam came around the back of the house. "I hear something," Mona gasped.

"Me, too," said Sheldon. "Sounds as if the cops are . . . *laughing.*"

"Come here and we'll show you your intruder, kids," one of the officers called. So we followed the police around to the back of the house.

A few moments later, Sheldon clapped me on the back, chortling, "Leave it to my sister, man!"

"But, but . . . ," I stammered. "What *is* that?"

"That's a life-size poster of Coach Joe Paterno," my twin cried. "Mr. and Mrs. Winch must be Penn State fans!"

I turned to Mona, asking, "Do you have any idea what he's talking about?" She shook her head, giggling too hard to answer. "Our intruder is a *poster*? I will never live this down. I'm sorry, Officers. You must think I'm an idiot."

"Not at all," one of them said. "You handled a difficult situation well, young lady. You might want to leave a note explaining why we were called."

"In case Mr. and Mrs. Winch hear about this from a neighbor before they've spoken to you," another officer said.

So that's what we did. By the time Mona drove back to our house, we'd abandoned any idea of going out. As Shel and Katherine and I went up the steps, I said, "Now remember, no one breathes a word of this to Mom. It will only worry her."

So what did my twin do the *minute* we walked in? He yelled, "Hey, Ma! Wait'll you hear what Abbey's done now!"

Instantly, she was at the top of the stairs, asking, "What's wrong?"

Sheldon's eyes widened as she came down the stairs. "You're home," he observed intelligently. "What are you doing *home*, Ma?"

All I could do was glare at him as she answered, "I have a meeting first thing in the morning, so Kevin brought me home early. And never mind me. Where have you three been?" Naturally, Sheldon had to tell her.

That was why I sat—crumpled, beaten, old before

my time—in the wing chair with my head in my hands, wailing, "But *Mo-om!*"

"I'm sorry, Abbey, but I don't want you putting yourself in potentially dangerous situations. I will go with you and Mona every night until Mr. and Mrs. Winch get home. Don't take any more jobs like this and don't argue with me."

I took my head out of my hands long enough to shoot a venomous look at Sheldon—who looked stricken, I had to admit.

Suddenly, our cousin spoke up. "Aunt Evelyn?"

"Yes, dear?"

"The police complimented Abbey on the way she handled the situation tonight. She called the Winches' house from here first before calling the police."

"Why did you do that, Abbey?" Mom asked.

"To see if maybe the person was supposed to be there," I answered. I was about to add that it was Katherine's idea.

But before I could, my cousin said, "Abbey thought she should call because if the man answered the phone, it meant he was supposed to be there."

"Pretty ingenious, don't you think, Ma?" Shel asked. "Naturally, it being a poster, there was no answer." He grinned when Mom started laughing.

Now, Shel knew as well as I did that if you could make Mom laugh, you were halfway home. That was one thing about our mother: She had a sense of humor.

"Mother?" I said, straightening up in my chair.

"Yes, Abbey."

"Haven't you raised me and Joyce to believe that women are just as capable as men?"

"Yes, but . . ."

"Well, the police thought I was extremely capable tonight, didn't they?" I looked at my brother and cousin.

"That's right," said Sheldon.

"They thought you were *très* capable," Katherine said, and winked.

I turned back to my mother, asking, "Have I ever caused you a moment's worry? *Serious* worry?"

"No, but . . ."

I held up my hand. "You have to let go of me, Mom. . . ." I ignored Sheldon, who stood behind her making shoveling motions. "You have to *trust* me. It's one of the hard things about being a parent; face it."

She opened her mouth to say something . . . and started laughing again. "I give up," she said. "You win, Abbey."

"Thanks," I said, and grinned as Sheldon whistled softly and Katherine applauded.

As Katherine and I got into bed a short time later, she said, "Abbey, there's something I'd like to know. Why did you tell Aunt Evelyn about tonight? Wouldn't it have saved trouble to make something up?"

I looked at her. "You mean lie?" I asked. She nodded. "We tell each other the truth in this family, Katherine."

"Always?" she asked.

"Always," I answered. That's when I remembered she'd said she'd tell me about this count person Aunt Claudia was living with. But right now, I was just too tired to listen.

Nine

The next day at the club, Rick came over to the chain-link fence surrounding the baby pool and called my name. The girls were sitting on the edge of the pool, happily kicking their feet in the water, so I picked up Cal and went over to talk to him.

"Thought I'd ask if you'd like to go out on the lake during my break this afternoon," he said. "There's a rowboat we can use."

"Sounds like fun," I said as Cathy and Cora came up. "But what about the kids?"

"Couldn't you leave them with another mother's helper?" he asked.

Cathy gripped my leg, saying, "Don't leave us! Don't leave us!"

"Don't worry, I won't." I patted her back. "I'm sorry, Rick, but the kids are my responsibility."

He studied me for a moment, then smiled. "If that's the only way you'll go, I guess the rug rats can come."

"I is not a rug rat," said Cal. Rick burst out laughing.

"Would you like to go in a boat on the lake?" I asked Cathy and Cora.

They nodded, their foreheads pressed to my leg. "But don't call us that," Cathy said into my thigh.

Rick leaned down to her, saying, "Okay, I won't!" Straightening up, he added, "I'll be over as soon as I go on my break, Abbey."

"See you then," I said. But I frowned as he walked away. Whoever heard of a lifeguard who didn't like kids? More importantly, if Rick didn't like kids, *how could I like him?*

"How'd it go with Rick today?" Joyce asked as soon as I got home that afternoon.

"So-so." I tossed her leopard-spotted hat onto the hall table.

"Nice hat head, Ab."

"Thanks," I said, returning her grin. "Rick took me and the kids for a row around the lake today. We saw two snapping turtles. The kids were thrilled."

"That sounds good. So how come you don't seem happier about it?" she asked.

"I'm starting to worry about myself, Joyce. Maybe I'm impossible to please." As we went out to the kitchen, I went on, "Rick's handsome, but I don't think he's my type."

"Why not, Ab?"

"I don't think he likes children very much."

"Does that make him a bad person?" she asked as I opened the refrigerator and stared glumly at the fruit amid the wide-open spaces.

"Brother, I'll be glad when Mom stops going out

with Mr. Macartney and goes back to buying junk food," I said, closing the door. "I don't think Rick's bad. I just don't think he's for me, that's all. I'm losing hope," I added, sitting down at the table. "Either the ideal man doesn't exist, or there's something wrong with me."

"Don't you think sixteen's a little young to give up, Ab? You know what Mom told me the other night? She said she was afraid she'd never find a man like Dad again, but she has. She says Kevin has a lot of Dad's best qualities, like the way he—"

I cleared my throat and picked up that morning's newspaper, asking, "Where's Katherine?"

After a moment, Joyce answered, "Taking a shower. I think she misses you since you started baby-sitting for the Costello kids, Abbey. She's mentioned a couple of times how busy you are."

"That's very flattering," I said as the phone rang.

Joyce got up to answer it. "Just a minute, please." She held the phone out to me. "For you, Ab."

"Hello?"

"Hi, Abbey."

"Oh, hi, Rick," I said as my cousin walked into the room. She wore a white terry-cloth robe, and her dark hair was slicked back, making her high cheekbones more noticeable. I put a hand to my face and sighed. They must've run out of cheekbones by the time they got to me, brother.

"You don't want to play volleyball?" Rick asked.

"Volleyball?"

"I just asked you to play with a group of my friends tonight," he said, "but you don't seem very enthusiastic."

"I'm not. I mean," I added, quickly, "I was thinking of something. I have a job checking a neighbor's house and—"

"I'll do it for you," Katherine said eagerly. "Please, Abbey."

"Who's that?" Rick asked.

"My cousin. She's living with us this summer. I guess I can play volleyball, after all. My cousin says she'll fill in for me."

"Great," he said. "I'll pick you up around seven. Better wear pants, Abbey. They're more comfortable when you're riding a motorcycle."

"I'm not allowed to, Rick. My mom has a thing about them."

"Oh," he said. "I'll ask my old man for the car then. Anyway, wear comfortable clothes, and bring a sweatshirt or something in case it gets chilly later. We usually sit around, sipping a few brews after the game."

"I don't drink," I said.

"You *don't?* Oh, well, you don't have to, I guess. So I'll see you at seven. Oh, and by the way . . ." His voice hung in the air. "I guess it's only fair to tell you, Abbey: We're playing at Melissa's house tonight. She's part of the group, you see. Well, I'll be by at seven. Ciao!"

"I can't even believe this," I said, sighing as I hung up.

"The bloom is definitely off the rose, huh, Abbey?" Joyce asked.

"Forget the bloom. It never got out of the bud stage, sports fans. Why can't I have a *normal* life?"

"I don't know," Katherine answered. "Maybe if you'd tell me what that phone call was about . . ."

"Okay." I pulled out a chair and sat down at the table. "Listen to this: I think the good-looking lifeguard at the Costellos' club is my ideal, right? Tall, dark, intelligent. Then I get to know him and realize I don't have much in common with him. Not only that, he pals around with an ex-girlfriend named Melissa, who hated me on sight."

"I'm starting to see that you and Shel are right about her," Katherine told Joyce. "She does tend to get dramatic about things, doesn't she?"

Joyce laughed. "Ab, I don't believe anyone could hate you."

Putting up a hand, I said, "Hear me out. Rick called to ask me to play volleyball with a bunch of people tonight, right? So, *after* I said I'd go, he informs me we're playing at Melissa's house!"

Joyce and Katherine looked at each other, then back at me. "So?" they said in unison.

"You guys are not being very supportive," I crabbed. "Melissa is this curvaceous blond who used to date Rick and still craves him. The first day I took the Costello kids to their club, she sought me out for the express purpose of telling me I didn't have a chance with Rick. Now I'm playing volleyball at her house?" I groaned, and put my head in my hands.

"Oh, Abbey," said Joyce, "you're overreacting. If Melissa gives you any trouble, just"—she shrugged —"ignore her. Right, Katherine?"

"*Mais oui, chérie,*" she said, smiling at my little sister.

Just wait until I tell Joyce and Katherine about this, I thought several hours later as Rick drove me home. So much for me overreacting about ex-girlfriends, brother.

"I'm sure you'll be all right in the morning," Rick told me for about the thousandth time since Melissa beaned me with the ball. "I'm sure it's nothing serious."

"Yeah, probably just a minor concussion," I said. "Actually, I don't think getting hit in the head was as bad as rolling down that hill and crashing into that bush. Just tell me one thing, Rick: Do you think Melissa did it on purpose?"

"Of *course* not," he said, horrified. "She's a very strong player, is all. Everyone got quite a kick out of you tonight, Abbey. They thought you were an awfully good sport."

"I'm awfully glad," I muttered, remembering their laughter as I spun out of control down that hill. Talk about adding insult to injury, brother.

"You're not much of an athlete, are you?" Rick asked. "Did I tell you that Melissa plays varsity volleyball for Colgate?"

Fortunately, we turned into my driveway at that

moment. I was almost home, almost away from this insensitive dolt.

He pulled up in front of the house and stretched his arm across the seat. "So, like to play again sometime, Abbey?" I was trying to come up with a polite but firm answer like *No, thanks* when he added, "If the others don't mind, that is. Some of us are quite serious about the game, you know."

That settled it. As I got out of the car, I thought, What a humorless toad this guy turned out to be.

As we went up the steps, I decided the only good thing about my throbbing head was that it gave me a good excuse not to kiss the toad good-night. Just to be certain, I groaned all the way up to the front door. I'll say one thing for Rick: He was a gentlemanly toad.

Thank heavens the house was quiet. No one had waited up. The last thing I needed was to explain why I looked as if I'd rolled down a grassy hill and crashed into a giant bush. My white shorts would never be the same, brother. I switched off the hall light and crept up the stairs.

There was a light on in our room. Good old Joyce had probably left it on for me. As quietly as I could, I let myself into the room.

"What happened to *you*?" Katherine whispered. She was sitting up in bed, a book open in her lap. "Abbey, you look terrible!"

I sighed. "Melissa spiked the ball into my head, I fell and rolled down a hill, all in front of a bunch of people from Yale, Harvard, Dartmouth, you name it. It was not a night to remember. I've got to go to bed. I've got a splitting headache."

"Do you want me to get you some aspirin?" she asked as I shed my shirt and shorts.

"I already took some," I whispered, carefully pulling on my nightgown. Then I got into bed and pulled the covers up over my head.

Ten

In the morning, my headache was pretty much gone, but I was still sore in body, not to mention spirit. How could I face Rick and Melissa after last night? But at the same time, how could I let Mrs. Costello and the kids down? I moaned and rolled over just as Joyce poked her little blond head into the room.

She immediately called, "Mom! Abbey's sick."

Good old Mom. She took one look at me and said, "You're not going to work today and that's that. I don't want to hear a word of argument." She stood at my bedside, looking like the firm, no-nonsense mother of my youth while Joyce and Katherine sat on the foot of my bed, looking concerned.

"If you say so," I said weakly. "But what about the Costello kids?"

"Let me go," Katherine piped up. "I'd be glad to fill in for you today, Abbey."

"What a wonderful idea," said Mom. "Thank you, Katherine. I'll call Nancy Costello to make sure it's all right with her. I'm going to call Dr. Willis, Abbey, just in case he wants to see you."

I popped up, saying, "I'm not *that* sick, for crying

out loud!" But she'd already left the room.

The upshot was that Mrs. Costello picked Katherine up and took her and the kids to the club while I went back to sleep for several hours. When I woke up, I felt as good as new.

Naturally, I called Mom at her office to report this miracle, and she said I didn't have to go to the doctor, after all. That was the good part of the day.

The bad part was that apparently the minute my former dream man spied Katherine at the Lake Club, he asked her out.

"I am crushed!" I cried, collapsing onto the couch.

"For a change," said Sheldon. "What's wrong now, dog face?"

"Katherine just called to ask if I'd mind if she went out with Rick Risteen tonight!"

"So? You just got finished regaling me with the story of your date last night, Ab. I believe you called this Rick guy a toad; am I right?"

"I know, but I'm *still* crushed. Rick could've at least given me the opportunity to turn him down the next time he asked me out."

"You're being a tad unreasonable, don't you think, Ab?"

"I can't help it." Crossing my arms over my chest, I groused, "It's humiliating. He asks me out one night and my younger cousin the next!"

"Ab." My twin gave me a look from under his blond brows.

"So what if I don't like him! Katherine's a mere

child, Sheldon! She's only thirteen! That's way too young for Rick. Don't you think a freshman in college is too old to date a thirteen-year-old?"

"Ordinarily, yes; but you have to admit, Ab, Katherine isn't like most thirteen-year-olds."

"Don't remind me." I sighed.

He grinned. "Don't tell me you're jealous of your own cousin."

I dropped my eyes. "Okay, so I'm a terrible person."

He chuckled, shaking his head. "You have no reason to be jealous of Katherine, Ab."

I threw my head back, saying, "*Ha!* Any girl would have reason to be jealous of Katherine! She makes me feel like a nerdy little mouse. A nerdy little short-haired mouse," I added, running a hand over my fuzzy head.

"You and Katherine are different types," Shel said. "There's no comparison between you, so why don't you stop comparing yourself to her?"

I gave him a look. "Okay, we know Katherine's the beautiful, suave type. What type am I?"

"The type who's got her act together, can laugh in the face of sorrow, and can be counted on when things get rough," he answered promptly.

"Gee, thanks," I said, touched. "I didn't know you thought about me like that."

"Man, oh, man, sometimes you act a little thick, Ab. Don't you realize that Katherine admires you?"

"No. I mean, I can tell she *likes* me and everything."

"What really bothers me about all this, Ab, is since when are you so concerned about your appearance, not to mention other people's?"

"Since I transformed my head into a coconut?" I asked. He broke up, making me smile in spite of myself. "Okay, I admit it, Shel. I've been a jerk lately."

"Y'see?" He got up from the wing chair and sat down next to me, slinging an arm around me. "That's one of the great things about you!"

I raised one eyebrow, waiting for the slam dunk. "Oh, what's that?"

"You *admit* it when you're a jerk."

"So you agree with me," I said.

"Yeah!" He nodded vigorously. "But don't feel too bad about it. Everyone acts like a jerk once in a while. I think maybe even *I* do."

"Not you, O golden one," I said, and started laughing. He did, too. He also ruffled my hair before jumping up and sprinting out of the room.

Eleven

An hour later, I was up in my room, reading, when I heard the roar of an engine. The Merritt Parkway ran past the house, so I was used to traffic sounds, but this was unusually loud.

Suddenly Joyce called, "Abbey, Shel, come here!"

We nearly collided in the hall. After hip-checking me out of his way, he raced down the stairs. I got down there just in time to see Katherine hop off the back of a motorcycle.

As good old Shel opened the door wide, he grabbed me, pulling me forward so that I could see Rick Risteen and he could see me standing there with my face hanging out. "Hi, Abbey!" he called, waving.

"Hi," I said, but I doubt he could hear as he revved his bike and yelled something to my cousin. Then he roared away down the driveway, and she came up the steps.

"Hello." She smiled at the three of us and shrugged out of her white windbreaker. Smoothing her short dark hair with her hand, she paused, looking at us. "Is something wrong?"

As if on cue, my brother and sister turned to me.

"Tell her about the rule, Ab," Shel ordered.

"What rule?" Katherine asked.

"We're not allowed to ride motorcycles," I answered. "Mom thinks they're dangerous."

"But they give one such a feeling of freedom!" She laughed, adding, "Besides, I'm allowed to ride them. I did all the time in France. Well, excuse me, I have to take a shower. Rick's picking me up at seven."

"So much for Katherine and rules," I muttered as she went upstairs.

"You'll have to talk to her after she's taken her shower," Shel said. "Tell her she can't go on motorcycles while she lives with us, and that's that."

"Why don't *you* tell her?" I asked. "How come I have to do it?"

But he was already headed up the stairs, whistling under his breath. "Don't worry, Ab," said Joyce. "We'll talk to Katherine together."

"But it's the *rule*," Joyce explained for the third time. "Don't you get it?"

Katherine's face darkened. She stuck out her chin, saying, "Frankly, I don't see what your rules have to do with me."

"Look," I said, "it's simple. While you live here, you have to—"

"Well, that's easy enough to fix!" She stood up, screwing the top back onto her bottle of nail polish. "I'll leave. Anytime; just let me know when it becomes too inconvenient to have me here." She plunked the nail polish down on the bureau before making her way between the bunks and my bed over to the closet.

"That's not what I meant, and you know it, Katherine," I said.

"Don't get mad at us," Joyce pleaded as Katherine whipped through the clothes in the closet, knocking hangers to the floor. She pulled out a short black cotton sheath as Joyce added, "Mom hates motorcycles, that's all. She thinks they're dangerous."

"Joyce, come here for a minute, will you?" I put my arm around her and led her out into the hall. "Maybe we better wait till Mom gets home and let her handle Katherine."

"Why is she so mad at us?" she whispered.

"Remember, she told you she didn't have rules where she used to live," I said. "And we've got another problem besides the motorcycle."

"What, Ab?"

"Katherine's too young for Rick Risteen. *I* think so, anyway."

Behind me, Katherine cried, "I knew it! You're jealous of me, aren't you, Abbey?" She stood in the doorway, her arms crossed over her chest.

"That's not it," I said. "That is absolutely not the point. Rick's in *college,* Katherine. He's—"

"You're blushing," she pointed out coolly. "And you can stop fretting, Abbey. I'll call him and tell him to pick me up in a car tonight." Putting her delicate nose in the air, she swept past us into Mom's room to use the phone.

As Joyce and I went downstairs, I said, "Now do you understand why I think we should let Mom handle her? She just thinks I'm jealous. Mom'll take care of Katherine. The minute she sees Rick, she'll realize he's too old for her and tell Katherine no way she's going out with him."

"I don't know," Joyce said, frowning. "Mom's kind of preoccupied these days. And I've noticed she doesn't treat Katherine the way she treats us. She treats her more like an equal."

"That's just because she still thinks of Katherine as a guest. Mom's always been strict," I added as we went out and sat on the front steps. "You'll see, Joyce. Mom'll treat Katherine just the way she treats us."

"I think you should tell Mom straight out how old Rick is," she insisted. "Mom didn't meet him when he came to get you last night, remember? She'd already gone out with Kevin."

"Well, if she'd stay home once in a while . . ." I began. I stopped when I saw the expression on Joyce's face. Just then, our beat-up old car came tooting down the driveway. "Here she comes now," I said. "You'll see, Joyce."

Mom got out of the car, calling, "Hi, girls! Your grandmother called me at the office this afternoon. She wants all of us to come over for dinner tonight."

"Yay!" Joyce cried, getting to her feet.

"I told Kevin I couldn't go out with him. It's been so long since the four of us have visited Gram together," Mom said as she came up the steps toward us.

"That's because Shel's always too busy to visit Gram," I said as we went into the house. "But *all* of us can't go tonight, Mom," I added, shooting a look at my sister.

"Oh?" Mom looked at me. "Who can't go?"

"Katherine," I answered. "She's going out—"

"With the same boy Abbey went out with last night," Joyce announced.

"He met her at the club when she filled in for me today," I explained just as the phone rang.

Upstairs, Shel yelled, "I'll get it!"

Mom waited until he'd thundered through the upstairs hall to ask, "Is your nose out of joint about this, Abbey?"

I felt my nose before answering, "No more than usual, I guess."

She smiled. "Good for you, dear."

"Tell her how old this boy is, Ab," Joyce prompted.

"He's eighteen, Mom. Too old for Katherine, don't you think?"

To my surprise, my normally strict, overprotective mother replied, "Not necessarily."

"I told you," said Joyce as I stared, horrified, at our mother.

"You mean you're going to let Katherine go out with him?" I asked. "Brother, you never would've let *me* go out with a college man when *I* was thirteen!"

"Did boys ask you out when you were that age?" she asked as Sheldon came bombing down the stairs.

"No," I admitted.

"Katherine strikes me as being very grown-up," said Mom as Sheldon slung an arm around my shoulders.

"Guess *what,* Ab?"

I rolled my eyes at him, asking, "*Must* I?" Joyce erupted into giggles.

"That was none other than *Bassett Hunter* on the phone, Ab!"

Bassett Hunter was a very nice guy who went to Fitchett Academy, the private day school Gram sends Shel to (so that he'll learn something instead of flirt with girls all day long). Anyway, last month, Bassett asked me to go to a couple of lacrosse games to watch him play. Then he asked me to go to a drive-in movie with him, and . . . let's just say that Bassett came on so strong, he scared me to *death.*

Still holding me in a viselike grip, Shel went on, "Guess what Bassett wanted, Ab. He wants me and you to come over to his house tonight!"

"That's nice, but—"

"He's having a whole bunch of people over, Ab. It's going to be *great,* man! I haven't seen a lot of those guys since school ended."

"I'm going over to Gram's with Mom and Joyce," I said, trying and failing to get away from him.

"You can still go," good old Mom said. "You two

can just excuse yourselves early. Your grandmother will understand."

"But I don't want to go to Bassett's," I said firmly. "Let *go,* Sheldon. Mom!"

"Aw, for crying out loud, dog face! You never want to do anything. You haven't done anything all summer. Ma, talk sense to her."

"I think you should go, Abbey," she said. "Shel, let her go."

"Certainly," he said, releasing me.

Mom turned back to me. "I want you to go tonight, Abbey. You'll have fun."

"Better wash your hair, though, Ab," Shel said, eyeing me. "You've got a wicked case of hat head." He chortled, skipping out of my reach as I lunged at him.

"All right, Abbey," Mom said, "stop horsing around and go take your shower. We have to get a move on. Your grandmother's expecting us. I'll tell Katherine what our plans are."

As I stomped up the stairs, Shel called after me, "Bassett will be real pleased, Ab!"

Forty-five minutes later, I got into the backseat of the car beside my sister. Mom sat in the passenger seat while Sheldon drove (for a change). All right, I thought as he drove down the driveway, so I'll accompany him to Bassett's, but it'll be the last time, brother!

"Just remember," I said as Shel turned onto Silverwood, "if Bassett starts calling me all the time again, it'll be your fault."

"If you get the opportunity tonight, Abbey," Mom said, "explain to Bassett that you'd just like to be friends with him."

"*Aargh!*" Shel yelled, making Joyce and me jump. "That's the worst, most hackneyed shoot-down there is, man!"

"It's not a shoot-down," said Mom. "All you have to do, Abbey, is explain to Bassett that you're not ready to go steady with one person. But be kind. Be friendly without encouraging him."

Suddenly, my precious little sister leaned her elbows on the back of the front seat and said, "Abbey's a little afraid of Bassett, and I don't blame her."

"Afraid?" Shel repeated.

"Uh, Joyce," I said, "don't—"

"You should hear what he did," she went on, ignoring me.

"Tell me, Joyce. I'll get Bassett if he—!" Shel began.

"Don't say another word," I ordered. "I mean it, Joyce."

"Quit digging your nails into my arm, Abbey," she said, rubbing her arm as Mom gave me a piercer over her shoulder.

"Maybe we should change the subject," Mom said, pointedly. "Did I tell you I've invited Kevin and his family to come for Sunday dinner this weekend, kids? I want you all on tap so you can meet everyone."

I was just about to ask who "everyone" was when Shel said, "Fine, Ma. Go on, Joyce. What'd Bassett do to Abbey?"

I gave her my sternest, no-nonsense look, and what was my formerly adored little sister's response? Her shoulders began heaving with silent hysterics. She blurted, "He tried to French-kiss her!"

I clapped my hand over her mouth just as Mom said, "All right, that's enough."

Meanwhile, the damage was done, sports fans. I resolved never to speak to anyone in my family again, except Gram.

So Shel and I went over to Bassett's, and I had a perfectly fine time. There were a lot of people there, and Bassett was so busy being a good host or whatever that I hardly saw him except to say hello when we first got there. Shel and I were home by midnight. Good thing. I was exhausted.

Hours later, something woke me up. At first I thought I was dreaming that someone was crying. But it went on until I realized I was awake and someone *was* crying.

I sat up in bed and squinted at the clock on the bureau. It was 3:15. That's when I remembered Katherine had gone out with Rick Risteen. Throwing back the covers, I got out of bed.

Boy, oh, boy, I thought, making my way across the dark room, I'll bet Mom's giving her holy heck, coming in this late. I stepped into the hall, being careful to avoid the squeaky floorboards.

That was one thing about Mom. She was very strict about what time you got in. Brother, was Katherine going to get it.

Flattening my body against the wall, I began sneaking down the stairs—just as my cousin started up. She stopped, looking shocked when she saw me. I raised a hand, saying, "Hi, there!"

"Abbey Reilly," Mom said, appearing at the foot of the stairs, "what are you doing?"

"I'll talk to you in the morning," Katherine whispered, passing me. Her hazel eyes were red and swollen from crying. Had Rick put the moves on my little cousin? Why, I'd give him a piece of my mind.

"Abbey?" Mom gestured for me to follow her into the living room. "I feel so bad for that poor child," she said, wrapping her rose-colored robe tightly around her as she sat down on the couch. "I just don't know what to do for her."

"I'll bet you read her the riot act for coming home so late, didn't you, Ma?"

"To tell you the truth, I didn't have the heart. They went to a party in New Canaan, and Katherine said she started telling the young man about her mother and . . ." She shook her head.

When she didn't say anything more, I asked, "You mean you didn't ground her for *life*? Mom, you would've killed *me* if I'd come in this late!"

"I know. But I'm sure Katherine needs someone to talk to. Did you know that she hasn't heard from her mother since she arrived here? I feel sorry for her. You have no idea what my sister is like, Abbey. She's just . . . Claudia has always been so wrapped up in her own life. My heart goes out to Katherine, poor little thing. That's why I was happy to have her with us this summer. She hasn't had much of a home life, I'm afraid."

I frowned. "I think we need to talk about what our responsibility is to Katherine, Mom."

She looked at me. "What do you mean?"

"If we care about her, shouldn't we treat her the same way we treat each other?"

"Well, of course."

"But we haven't been, Mom. For instance, you wouldn't have let me go out with a freshman in college when I was her age."

"You're probably right. . . . But Katherine is very grown-up," she said tiredly.

"Maybe she isn't, though. Maybe she just *looks* grown-up, so people treat her as if she is. Maybe it isn't so great to look older than you are."

"Maybe," Mom agreed, trying and failing not to yawn. "Right now all I'm sure of is that I've got to go to bed, and so do you."

Twelve

I waited for Rick Risteen to seek me out the next day. I figured he'd want to pump me about Katherine, so that morning I'd practiced smiling at myself in the bathroom mirror, saying in a sincere tone, "I'm so glad you and my cousin hit it off!"

Sure enough, after lunch he came over to the baby pool to talk. But instead of pumping me for information about what Katherine thought of him, he shook his head, saying, "Too bad about your cousin, Abbey."

I took my eyes off the kids splashing around in the pool long enough to give him a quizzical look. "What's too bad?"

"She's so loused-up. I'm not attracted to screwed-up girls, even ones as pretty as your cousin."

"Calvin, don't push people, honey," I called. Turning back to Rick, I asked, "Who says she's screwed-up?"

"She did, in so many words. She told me all about her mother marrying that lord or whatever he is. I mean, give me a break! I want to *hear* all this stuff?"

"He's a count, and Aunt Claudia's not married to him."

"Whatever," he said. "She's going to marry him, and Katherine's all messed-up about it."

"I guess my cousin's so young and inexperienced that she thought you might be interested in hearing about it," I said in a casual tone.

"Hey, life is tough, Abbey. Who wants to listen to someone else's problems? I mean, bor-ing." He flapped his hand. Then he gave me the full effect of his dazzling smile, asking, "So, how've *you* been?"

"Just fine," I replied evenly, as Cathy and Cora raced over to me to escape a small boy wielding a squirt gun.

I couldn't believe it. Rick blew his dumb whistle and yelled, "You're all benched for ten minutes! Any more running today, I close this pool! So," he said, turning back to me, "how about going to a movie one night this weekend?"

"You girls go over and sit on your towels," I said. "I'll be right there." As they walked carefully away, I graced Rick with one of my better fake smiles. "To tell you the truth, I think I'm going to be too busy spending time with my cousin this weekend. She's just a kid, and I guess she needs someone to talk to." Before he could respond, I turned on the soles of my rubber thongs and walked away.

"He's a poop head," Cora said as I sat down next to her. "Why do you like a poop head, Abbey?"

I opened my mouth to scold her, but then I

thought better of it. Putting my arm around her shoulders, I asked, "Who said I did?"

She grinned and patted my knee, saying, "I *like* you."

"I like you, too, kid."

Thirteen

Sunday afternoon, Katherine and I were out in the kitchen, preparing hors d'oeuvres for Mr. Macartney and his family. Or rather, Katherine sat on the counter, watching me wrap baby hot dogs in dough (which she called *saucisses en croûte*).

Suddenly she said, "Aunt Evelyn is serious about this man, *n'est-ce pas?*"

"She spends a lot of time with him, but it's no big deal."

She laughed. "Don't be silly. Anyone can see *c'est l'amour.*"

"Will you stop that?" I snapped.

Her smile faded. "Stop what?"

"Throwing in French phrases. It's a little affected, don't you think?" I shoved the cookie sheet into the oven.

"I beg your pardon," she said stiffly. "I *am* bilingual, you know."

She reminded me so much of Joyce, poking her lower lip out like that, that I almost smiled. "Oh, don't pay any attention to me today," I told her. "I'm feeling grouchy is all. But this thing with my mother and Mr. Macartney is not true *l'amour.* It's certainly not what she had with my father. She's never going to feel that way about anyone, ever again."

"I never said she would, Abbey. That was a unique love affair."

I looked at her. "You realized that when you were a little kid?"

She nodded. "My mother envied your parents' marriage, you know. She once said it was made in heaven."

"That's what I always thought, too."

"I loved visiting you when we were little," she said, sounding wistful. "I used to pretend your mother and father were . . . my parents."

Suddenly I felt bad for her. "They would have been flattered if they'd known, Katherine."

"Did I tell you about the book I found that Uncle Rob must have given to your mother?"

"No. How do you know Dad gave it to Mom?" I asked.

"The inscription . . . it's very romantic."

The expression on her face was so radiant, I had to look away. I busied myself, getting the hors d'oeuvres out of the oven, putting them on a plate. Finally I asked, "Will you find the book for me later? I'd like to see it."

"Of course."

I started to leave the kitchen, then stopped. "Katherine? Rick told me about your mother marrying the count."

She looked stricken. "He did?"

I nodded. "How come you didn't tell me?"

She shook her head. "I can't live with a man like that, Abbey. I don't want Aunt Evelyn to know . . . what happened."

"What happened?" I repeated in a hushed voice.

"I can't tell you now. You'd better serve the hors d'oeuvres before they cool. Go on," she said, almost smiling. "And stop looking so worried. I'll bring out the second batch when they're ready."

"Thanks. You're not such a helpless little petunia anymore, you know that, Katherine? This family must be shaping you up."

"A helpless little petunia? Is *that* what I was?" she asked. As I started to leave the room, she added, "Well, *you* look more chic since I cut your hair, *Abernathy*." She shrieked and jumped off the counter as I rushed her.

In the hall, I pressed my lips together to stop giggling. Mom had given us strict instructions to be on our best behavior in front of the Macartneys. Taking a deep breath, I smoothed my close-cropped hair and pulled down the red top I'd borrowed from Katherine. Then I proceeded into the living room, where our guests awaited.

Our awaiting guests certainly were making a racket. Everyone was talking and laughing at once. I frowned. It sounded as if they were having fun.

Brother, what a scene, I thought, pausing in the archway. Mr. Macartney's four-year-old granddaughter, Sophie, was climbing the back of the couch in spite of Joyce and Sheldon's efforts to interest her in a puzzle. The two-year-old, Nora, stood on a chair, systematically removing the books from the bottom shelf of the bookcase.

Meanwhile, the adults were oblivious. Mom was talking a mile a minute to Mr. Macartney's mother and daughter, Phyllis, while Mr. Macartney talked to his son-in-law, Sam Elksnits. As I entered the room, Shel and Joyce gave up on Sophie and started doing the jigsaw puzzle themselves. Meanwhile, Nora hopped off the chair and kicked off her ballet slippers (the Macartneys had come over directly from the little girls' ballet recital).

"Thank you, Abbey," the ladies said, helping themselves to the hors d'oeuvres.

"You're welcome. Mrs. Elksnits? Nora's trying to—"

"These are delicious!" Mrs. Elksnits cried, popping another hot dog into her mouth.

"Abbey and my niece made them," Mom told her.

"You're blessed, Evelyn," said Mrs. Macartney. "May I, dear?"

"Certainly," I said, holding the plate out to her again. "Uh, Mrs. Elksnits?"

"Now, Abbey," she said, biting into another hors d'oeuvre, "I insist you call me Phyllis. Mrs. Elksnits is my mother-in-law." For some reason, all three women found this quite hilarious.

As I passed the hors d'oeuvres to the men, I

thought that if *I* had a last name like Elksnits, I guess I'd rather be called by my first name, too. You'd really have to love a guy to take on a name like that, brother.

That's when I noticed Nora again. She'd gotten her scratchy pink tutu off and was working on her tights. Clearing my throat, I tapped my mother on the shoulder. "Excuse me, Mom, but—" My voice trailed off when I noticed how she and Mr. Macartney were smiling at each other.

"Let me help, Abbey!" Phyllis cried, getting up. "You've worked all afternoon."

I handed her the plate, saying, "Thanks, Mrs.—I mean, Phyllis. Uh, Nora seems to be—"

"Aren't these delish, Granny?" she cried, passing the tray.

I tugged at her sleeve. "Phyllis, Nora's strip—"

But she was too busy telling Mom, "You're just wonderful to have all of us to dinner, Evelyn."

"It's our pleasure," said Mom, smiling away as Mr. Macartney patted her hand.

I made one last try. "Mom, Nora's taking off her—"

"Most people wouldn't have included small children," Phyllis went on.

"It wouldn't be nearly as much fun without them," Mom murmured.

"Of course, this house is perfect for children," Mrs. Macartney remarked, looking around at our worn brown couch, the scruffy wing chair, and the scarred coffee table. "This room looks well lived in, well loved."

"Why, thank you, Mrs. Macartney," said Mom, pleased.

Good old Nora was down to her diaper by this time. As she pranced around the couch, I tapped Mr. Macartney on the shoulder, saying, "Excuse me, but Nora's trying to tell you something."

He burst out laughing. I had to laugh, too. She was a cute little brunette, with a wicked gleam in her dark eyes.

"I wish I still had some of Joyce's baby clothes, but I gave everything away when we moved to Connecticut," Mom said.

"I should have thought to bring a change of clothing," Phyllis said, taking Nora from her grandfather. I helped get her back into her tights and tutu.

When Nora started crying, Mom said, "Why don't you older kids take the little ones outdoors for a while, Abbey?"

So I picked up Nora, and Shel and Joyce each took one of Sophie's hands.

As we filed out of the room, Phyllis exclaimed, "You're *marvelous* with children, Evelyn!"

"If she's so marvelous with children, how come *we're* taking care of them?" Sheldon said, sotto voce. I snorted with laughter just as Katherine came out of the dining room with the second batch of hors d'oeuvres.

"Where are all of you going?" she asked.

"The natives are getting restless," Shel answered, just as Sophie wrapped her arms around his knees. "Soph? I can't move, Soph. Help!" he said. Sophie cracked up.

In the living room, I heard Mrs. Macartney say, "And your children are wonderful with the little ones, too. You've certainly done a good job with your three, my dear."

"Can I come?" Katherine asked as Shel pried Sophie off and picked her up.

"No," I answered, and grinned. "What a question! Ditch those hors d'oeuvres and come on."

It was one of those perfect summer days, warm but not hot, fragrant with freshly mown grass. The minute Shel and I put the little girls down, they shrieked and took off around the house.

"Let them go," said Sheldon. "There's nothing in the backyard to hurt them. Jeez, let them burn off steam."

Joyce grinned, saying, "I always wanted a little brother or sister."

"Indeed!" said I. "You mean Shel and I weren't enough?"

Katherine started laughing.

"I wanted someone I could *boss*," Joyce explained.

Shel turned on her. "Are you suggesting that Abbey and I bossed *you*?"

She rolled her eyes at Katherine, saying, "He drives me crazy when he does that."

"Does what?" our cousin asked.

"Asks obvious questions," Joyce replied.

We rounded the corner of the house and stopped to watch Sophie and Nora, twirling slowly under the trees, dancing in their pink tutus. When Shel nudged me, I put a finger to my lips. The four of us stood there, watching silently.

I bit my lip, trying not to remember being that young, that unconscious of how funny and beautiful you are. But the memory of an afternoon very like this one came to me.

I was sitting in the grass with my father, leaning heavily against him, my ear pressed to his back, saying, "Talk to me, Dad. I love the way your voice sounds." It sounded, to my childish ears, like the voice of God.

Now, Sheldon slapped me on the back. "Quit daydreaming and pay attention, Ab. We're going to play hide-and-seek, and guess who's It!"

I propped my hands up on my hips. "Not *me*, bozo."

He widened his brown eyes, saying, "But it was a unanimous decision. We took a vote while you were standing around *mooning*."

"I was not!"

"Were, too," he contradicted, and clapped his hands. "All right, girls, Abbey's It! Everybody hide while It counts to ten. Start counting, It," he ordered, grabbing me as I prepared to go off in a huff. "And no fair peeking. Hurry, girls, *hide* before It finishes counting! Hurry up," he called, whipping the little girls into a frenzy of shrieking tulle.

As Shel took off after them, I thought, Why fight it? You know he won't leave you alone. So I began counting. "One, two, three . . ." Finally I yelled, "Ready or not, here I come!" I turned around.

Joyce and Katherine were sitting there, looking at me.

"You were supposed to hide, guys," I said.

Joyce looked at Katherine. "We're a little old for hide-and-seek, *n'est-ce pas?*"

"*Oui, chérie.* As American teenagers say, *like, quel* fun." Katherine started to yawn, and burst into giggles.

"All right, you guys," I said. "We all know Shel's probably cheating. He probably took the little kids inside or something."

"Let's fake him out and go up to our room," Joyce suggested.

"Good idea," said Katherine.

As we headed toward the house, I said, "I wish Gram would hurry up and get here. Shel always behaves himself around Gram."

Joyce screamed as a small head suddenly poked out from under the bush by the back door. There was a brief but violent struggle, then Sophie crawled out from under the bush and got to her feet. The pink tutu looked as if it had been through a cyclone.

"*Soph!*" the bush hissed. "You're not supposed to come out yet!"

She bent down and peered into the shrubbery.

Straightening up again, she announced, "They're still in there!"

"They sure are," I said. "I'd know Shel's beady brown eyes anywhere. Come out, come out wherever you are," I deadpanned. The bush broke up. A moment later, he crawled out with little Nora in tow.

Before he could stand up, I plunked Sophie onto his back, saying, "Now we're playing ride-the-horsey!"

"Me, me!" Nora shrieked, so I put her on "Horsey's" back, too. Joyce, Katherine, and I yelled encouragement as Shel neighed and staggered around the backyard on his hands and knees while the girls screamed with glee.

Suddenly, Sophie collapsed, letting her arms dangle on either side of Shel's head. "Gweat game, Shel, but I'm tired now."

"Thank you, Lord." He sighed as the little girls slid off him. "I'll get you for this, Ab," he added just as Mom stuck her head out the back door and called Katherine to the phone.

As Katherine ran inside, Shel said, "Okay, you guys, I just thought of *another* neat game. It's called . . . rake-up-last-year's-leaves!"

"Yay!" the little girls squealed, jumping up and down.

"See that, Ab? They love the idea," said Sheldon. "You and Joyce better go get the rakes out of the garage."

"Ab?" Joyce said as I raised the garage door a short time later.

"Boy, oh, boy, we'll never find anything in here."

"You've got to give Shel credit, Ab."

"For what?" I pulled a rake out of a pile of garden tools. "Help me find the other rake, will you?"

She lifted an old bike, revealing the second rake. "He's a genius when it comes to getting other people to do his work," she said. "A couple of days ago, I heard Mom tell Shel she wanted him to get rid of that leaf pile in the back."

I gasped and dropped the rake. *"Sheldon."*

"Abbey?" Katherine ran down the front steps as Joyce and I came out of the garage. "My mother's coming next weekend!"

Fourteen

Katherine's hazel eyes shone with joy. She pushed a lock of hair out of her eyes; the breeze pushed it back. For once, I thought how pretty she was without feeling that awful twinge that made me feel bad about myself. "That's terrific," I said. "Is she bringing—?" I was about to say "the count," but she frowned and shook her head.

"She just got into New York. She's visiting friends before coming here. . . . Oh, I am so happy!" She threw her arms wide just as Gram's car came down the driveway and Sophie and Nora scampered around the house, followed by Shel. Mom, Mr. Macartney, his mother, and the Elksnitses came to the front door when Gram tooted the horn.

"What a lovely reception!" Gram said, laughing, hugging Joyce as the little girls wiggled around. "Hello, Evelyn. Sorry I'm late." She kissed my mother, asking, "Who have we here?"

"These are Kevin's granddaughters," Mom answered. "Aren't they darling?"

Then Mom introduced Gram to Mr. Macartney's

family and everyone started chatting and laughing as Nora and Sophie cavorted around. I was standing a little apart from everyone when I heard Mr. Macartney murmur, "What a wonderful family we're going to have, sweetheart."

No one noticed the way he took her hands, no one noticed the way they looked at each other . . . except me.

As the breeze carried the faint wail of a train whistle to my ears, Mr. Macartney drew my mother to him and kissed her on the lips.

Then Katherine was beside me, whispering, "Oh, Abbey, I'm so happy!"

And Gram was saying, "How are you today, my pet?"

Without taking my eyes off Mom and Mr. Macartney, I said, "That's great about your mom, Katherine. I'm fine, Gram. How're you?"

She stroked my cheek, forcing me to look at her. Her bright blue eyes were full of understanding as she put her arm through mine.

"Can we do this again next Sunday, Aunt Evelyn?" Katherine asked as we turned toward the house. "I want Claudia to meet everyone."

"I don't see why not," Mom answered. "What do you think, Kevin?"

"It's a grand idea," he answered, smiling into her eyes.

"We'd love to come," Phyllis said. "I'll find a sitter for the kids next time. . . ."

"Don't you dare," said Mom. "We want the whole family together. . . ." She paused, turning pink.

"As long as we're all together now, darling," Mr. Macartney said gravely, "why put off our announcement any longer?"

Shel's and my eyes met. His face was expressionless, but a muscle twitched in his jaw. "What's up, Ma?" he asked, and his voice cracked.

I didn't have to ask. I knew why she blushed and bit her lip. How could you? I thought, blinking back tears. How could you stand there looking so young and foolish? *So in love.*

Even though I knew what was coming, my stomach flipped as Mr. Macartney announced, "Evelyn and I are going to be married, everyone."

Before anyone else could react, Joyce said, "Oh, *goody.*" And everyone laughed.

"That's wonderful," Gram said, as if she meant it. "I'm very, very happy for you, Evelyn, my dear."

As my grandmother hugged Mom, Shel rubbed his hands off on the seat of his khakis and went over to shake Mr. Macartney's hand. Then Phyllis kissed my mother and Mom kissed Mrs. Macartney . . . and everyone turned to me.

"Congratulations, Mr. Macartney," I said. "That's great, Mom."

As I shook hands with Mr. Macartney, he said, "I wish you'd call me Kevin now, Abbey."

I said, "I'll try, Mr. Macartney," and everyone laughed again.

*   *   *

As soon as our company was gone and the kitchen was clean, I went upstairs and shut myself up in the closet. That was the best place to be when I was ashamed of myself.

I don't know how long I'd been in there when there was a knock on the door. Sheldon, I thought, glaring at the crack of light under the door.

"Abbey?" Katherine said softly. "I know you're in there and I just want to say that I know how you feel. When Claudia told me she was going to marry the count, I wanted to run away, or jump out a window. . . ."

"You did?" I blurted. "Brother, talk about overreacting," I said, and felt a smile pulling at my mouth. I stood up and opened the door. "You idiot," I said, smiling at her.

"When I think back on it, I'm embarrassed at how childishly I behaved."

"I can't imagine you acting childish, Katherine."

"You don't know everything about me, Abbey, even if we are cousins. I just wanted to say, if you need someone to talk to, I'm here."

"Thanks." I sat down on my bed as she sat on the bottom bunk. "What's the big mystery about the man your mother's going to marry?"

She paled, dropping her eyes. "Something happened, and I can't talk to Claudia. . . . I just told her I won't live with him, ever. That's why she asked if I could live here this summer."

"You mean you didn't come because she's out of a job?"

She shook her head. "That was just what she told Aunt Evelyn."

"Why did she lie to my mother, her own sister?"

"She doesn't want your mother to know that I refused to live with the man she was living with."

"Katherine, I imagine horrible things about this man. . . . You keep saying you're going to tell me, but you don't."

Her hazel eyes darkened. She glanced at the doorway, then back at me. "You have to promise you won't tell your mother," she said quickly. "Promise, or I won't tell you."

"I promise," I whispered.

"We were staying in his villa, and one night he and my mother went to a party. They came home very late. I heard them come in. . . . He came into my room, Abbey. He sat on my bed."

I stared at her for a moment. Then I said, "Maybe he'd had too much to drink and went into the wrong room."

She gave me a look that said, You child, you. "He was stroking my face when I woke up, Abbey. He tried to kiss me."

I gasped. "I would've screamed bloody murder!"

She almost smiled, saying, "I did. Naturally, he left rather quickly."

"I think you should tell your mother," I said. "I really do."

"I can't. I'm afraid to. That night, I told her I had had a bad dream."

"But why?" I whispered.

"I was afraid," she said again. "What if she accused me of lying?" Her voice was calm, but there was pain in her eyes.

I started to say, "She wouldn't." But then I thought, Maybe Aunt Claudia would. She'd lied to my mother, hadn't she? Why wouldn't she think Katherine was capable of telling her a lie?

"Or what if she'd gotten angry and confronted the count?" Katherine went on. "You know he would've denied it. *Then* where would I be? Would Claudia believe me . . . or him? If she believed me, would the engagement be broken? If so, what then?"

I grimaced. "Your mother might blame you?"

She nodded, saying, "You're beginning to understand."

"I guess I am."

She stood up and held out a book I hadn't noticed earlier. "This is the book I told you about, the one Uncle Rob gave your mother."

I took it from her and waited until she'd left the room to read the inscription in my father's generous scrawl:

> *To Evelyn, my beloved:*
> *Shy one, shy one,*
> *Shy one of my heart,*
> *She moves in the firelight*
> *Pensively apart.*

"Abbey!" Shel yelled up the stairs. "Mona's on the phone!"

"What's wrong?" I asked as soon as I heard her voice. "I can tell you're upset about something."

"Crystal Glass is the one who's upset. She's home, Abbey."

"You mean here in Connecticut? I thought she was spending the summer with her father on the West Coast, Mona."

"She was, but she came home because she's worried about her mother. I guess Mrs. Glass has been pretty upset having Crystal gone. She says her mom needs her. Anyway, she called me about running early tomorrow morning and she asked me to ask you if you'd like to run with us. I know Crystal's not one of your favorite people, Ab. . . ."

"What, just because she made me lose that track meet last spring?"

"You mean you're not mad at her anymore?" she asked, sounding hopeful.

"I think maybe I'm growing up, Mona," I said. "I don't have time to hold a dumb grudge when I have so many good things in my life."

"You're so great," she said, sighing. "I'll call Crystal and tell her you'll be at the intersection of Perry and Silverwood tomorrow morning. Thanks, Ab."

"For what?"

"For being a friend . . . to me and Crystal."

Fifteen

I swear, you would've thought the queen of England was coming to visit the way everyone in my house behaved during the next week. I got home from baby-sitting the Costello kids every afternoon to find my sister and cousin swabbing down the floors, washing curtains and walls, something.

On Friday night, we all went to the train station to meet Aunt Claudia. She stepped off the 6:15 wearing a bronze-colored raincoat against the slight drizzle, and I doubt there was one commuter getting off with her who didn't smile at her.

Nobody took much notice of us kids or Mom. It was funny. She and Aunt Claudia resembled each other—both were small with good figures, dark-blond hair, and brown eyes—but Aunt Claudia had *glamour.* Next to my quiet, little mother, Aunt Claudia was like a stunning jewel.

Now it was almost eleven on Saturday morning, and the jewel had just woken up.

"I always make her breakfast in bed when we're together," Katherine said, searching the kitchen cupboards. "Do you have any tea? Claudia doesn't drink coffee."

"Sure. In there." I nodded at the canister on the counter.

She opened it and looked aghast. "Oh, dear. Don't you have anything besides Lipton, Abbey?"

"Nope," I answered, filling the kettle. "That's it, kid."

"Well, it'll have to do," she said doubtfully. "Claudia always has a fresh croissant in the morning."

"It's a little late now, don't you think?" I asked. "I really don't think it would be a hot idea to call Mom in her *office* on a *Saturday* to ask her to pick up fancy tea and fresh croissants for Aunt Claudia's breakfast in bed, do you?"

She bit her lip. "That would be a very, very bad thing to do, wouldn't it?"

"*Oui*," I replied. She laughed. "There's a loaf of whole wheat in the bread box. Your mom will just have to make do with good old toast like the rest of us peons."

"It'll be a new experience for her," she said, her eyes sparkling. "Claudia will just have to *deal with it,* as you say; right, Abbey?"

"Right. Hey, Katherine, why didn't the count come with your mom?"

She put bread in the toaster and pushed it down carefully before answering, "She hasn't mentioned him. I'm hoping she's no longer seeing him."

"*Seeing* him?" I repeated. "She lives with him and plans to marry him."

"Maybe it's over," she said, sounding so hopeful it

broke my heart. "It's happened before, after all."

"How many times has she been engaged?"

"Twice that I know of," she answered.

I watched her as she bustled around, fixing her mother's breakfast. Finally, I said, "Well, if you ever want to talk about it, you know where to find me."

"We're starting to sound alike," she said. "I believe I said that to *you* just last weekend."

I returned her smile. "You did," I said, and left the room.

Aunt Claudia was sleeping in my bed while she was here, so I was camped out on the living room couch. Now I took my time, folding and putting away the sheets and whatnot so that Katherine could have some time alone with her mother. After stashing a few stray articles of clothing under the couch and arranging the magazines on the coffee table in a fan shape, I decided I couldn't put off getting dressed any longer and went upstairs.

As I walked into the room, I thought how lucky it was that Mom had to work today. I think the sight of my pretty aunt wearing an ivory satin bed jacket, propped up against what looked like every pillow in the house, and having breakfast in bed, might have irritated my hardworking mother just a bit.

"Sorry to interrupt," I said, "but I need to get some clothes."

"You're not interrupting at all, Abbey," Aunt Claudia said graciously. "I appreciate your moving out of your bed for me, lovie."

"As the French would say, *c'est ne rien!*" I said, and grinned at Katherine. But I don't think she heard. She sat on the end of the bed, picking glumly at the bedspread.

As I made my way over to the dresser, Aunt Claudia asked, "Aren't you excited about Evelyn getting married again?"

Katherine shot her mother such a look that I paused as I opened a drawer. Was that anger or sorrow, I wondered as my cousin stood up, saying, "You'd better have a bath and get dressed before Aunt Evelyn gets home, Claudia."

Her mother caught her hand. "What shall we do for fun this afternoon, dear heart? We could go shopping. You could do with some new things. You're looking a little shabby, my sweet."

"I borrowed these cutoffs from Abbey. American teenagers don't need anything more than jeans and T-shirts to bum around in," Katherine said stiffly. Then she pulled her hand out of her mother's grasp and left the room.

"Bum around in?" Aunt Claudia repeated, forcing a laugh. Then she looked at me. "Will you talk to her for me? Please?"

"About what?" I asked, as if I didn't know.

Her face lit up, reminding me of Katherine. "I'm getting married again, too, you know!"

I nodded. "Katherine told me about the count, Aunt Claudia."

Her smile faded. "What *do* you girls want for us?"

she asked. "Do you expect your mothers to remain single until *you* get married?"

"I never thought of it like that," I admitted. When she started weeping quietly, I left.

A few minutes later, I found Katherine in the kitchen, swabbing down the counter. She looked at me briefly before going back to her scrubbing. "She's all upset," I said. "Maybe you should go talk to her."

She sighed and closed her eyes for a moment. Then, "What is there to talk about? I can't live with the man my mother plans to marry . . . not that she wants me with her, you understand."

"Oh, Katherine, that's a terrible thing to—"

"But it's true," she said so firmly that I shut my mouth. "She doesn't want me; I know that. I've known it forever. Why do you think I've always stayed with 'friends' while Claudia worked? Don't you think she could've taken me with her some of the time, Abbey?"

I shook my head. How could I answer questions like that? "You can stay here," I said.

"Thank you, Abbey. You're very dear . . . but I can't. Aunt Evelyn's getting married again. I *wouldn't* do that to her."

"But—"

"Don't," she said gently. "Please don't worry about it. You have to understand that I've lived with lots of people. . . . I'm used to this."

"But I know once we explain the situation to Mom, she'll—"

Her face darkened. *"You promised,"* she said. "I will never forgive you if you—"

"Katherine, calm down. I'll just tell Mom that Aunt Claudia doesn't . . ." I hesitated.

"Doesn't want her only child? *Mon dieu.*" She covered her eyes, laughing a little. "Think what an uproar there'd be if you ever told Aunt Evelyn that. Claudia would go out of her mind if anyone even suggested it! It doesn't matter that it's true."

"But you can't just *leave*," I said. "We're just starting to get used to having you around! I'm teasing," I added hastily as her face fell. "I'm kidding you the way I would Joyce or Shel. We *like* having you—"

"Yes," she said, "I've heard that before."

"But you're *family*. Family is different."

"Yes," she said again. "Family certainly is different." Before I could stop her, she left the room.

That afternoon, I thought about my cousin's situation as I walked up to Mona's house (good old Sheldon had swiped the car as soon as Mom got home). And I decided I could talk to Mona about Aunt Claudia's remarriage without breaking my promise to Katherine.

After giving Mona some of the background, I asked, "What should I say to convince Katherine it's fine if she stays with us?"

"I'm not sure words will do it, Ab. Maybe action is the only thing that's going to convince her. From what you tell me, she's never really lived with her mom, so . . ." She shrugged. "Why would she think your family would want her any more than her own mother?"

"Good question," I said, sighing.

"What are you going to do?" she asked, walking me to the front door.

"I haven't decided yet, but I'll let you know."

As soon as I got home, Joyce nailed me. "Ab? How would you like to help your favorite little sister out?"

I laughed. "My favorite little sister, huh?"

"I want you to know I took it to heart when you told me that running track taught you to set goals for yourself," she said.

I crossed my arms. "And?"

"And I've set one for myself, Ab. All because *you* taught me the importance of setting goals. I want you to know that I listen when you talk. That's why," she hurried on as I started laughing, "I set a goal to sell five hundred boxes of assorted greeting cards by September first."

"Five hundred boxes of—? Are you *crazy*? We don't know that many people, Joyce!"

"But I have to earn money to buy Mom a wedding present . . . a good one." Tears filled her eyes. "It's important to me."

"Oh, Joyce . . ." I threw a pleading glance at Sheldon as he came in the door.

"I already ordered five hundred boxes, Ab. You

have to help me," she said, starting to cry.

Shel began to laugh, but I gave him such a look that he stifled it. "All right, don't worry," I said, patting her. "I'll help you."

It was like the sun breaking through the clouds. "Thanks, Ab! So, how're we going to sell five hundred boxes of cards by September first?"

"Are you two out of your *minds?*" Sheldon cried.

"We can do it," I replied as Joyce stuck her tongue out at him. "We can do anything we really put our minds to, right, Joyce?"

"Right!" she said, throwing her arm over my shoulder. That's when I turned and caught a glimpse of Katherine standing at the top of the stairs.

I started to say, "Come join us," but she disappeared down the hall.

Sixteen

As soon as Aunt Claudia left, Katherine seemed to withdraw. She appeared for meals, but stuck to herself otherwise.

So I was glad when R & R Service got a call to wash windows on Friday. It gave me the opportunity to ask Katherine to take over watching the Costello kids for a day. I figured work was good for the soul. At the very least, it would get her mind off her mother's remarriage.

"What's up with your cousin these days?" Mona asked as we washed windows side by side that afternoon. "You haven't mentioned her lately, Abbey."

"Can you read minds?" I asked as I pulled the top part of the window out so that I could clean the outside pane. "I was just thinking about Katherine. I overheard her telling Mom last night that she might go to live with a friend of the family in New York this fall."

"Eavesdropping again?" she asked, giving me a sideways look. I laughed. "How come Katherine's not going back to Europe to live with her—?"

"The only 'friend' of the family I know of in New York," I said, cutting her off, "is her father, and she's never even met him."

"Are you serious?" Mona asked. "What did your mother say to Katherine about this?"

I sighed, shaking my head. "She said that whatever Katherine wanted was fine with her. Which really isn't like Mom—let's face it, Mona. She's just so wrapped up in her own life these days."

She paused to look at me. "Maybe your mother would prefer that Katherine leave, Abbey, so your family can get back to normal."

"That's just it," I said. "Having Katherine with us has become normal. I've learned that this summer. Wherever you happen to be in life is what normal is. You have to deal with it instead of whining and wishing for things to get back to what *was*."

"You wouldn't also be talking about your mom getting married again, would you?"

"Possibly," I admitted. "It kills me, all the time I've wasted waiting for Mom to stop dating Mr. Macartney so we could get back to normal. Now 'normal' is going to be having a father again. A step-father, I mean."

Mona patted my shoulder. "It'll be okay," she said. "I'm sure of it."

"Thanks, Mona."

"Your cousin is lucky she has you guys. What if the only family she had was her parents?"

I nodded, saying, "I've been thinking a lot about families lately, and not just because of Katherine's situation. Because mine is about to change, I guess. I get really nervous and clutched-up, but then I think of Mr. Macartney's grandchildren. You should see them, Mona. They're wild! Shel and Joyce get a big kick out of them, too. We get down on our hands and knees to play with those little girls." I bit my lip, asking, "Do you think we're immature or something?"

She chuckled. "I think you're wonderful, Ab." Then she wiped the smile off her face, saying, "Now tell me the truth about why your cousin isn't going home to her mother. There must be more to the story than you've told me."

I sprayed glass cleaner and began wiping a new pane before answering, "I can't tell you why, Mona. I promised I wouldn't."

Mona nodded. After a moment, she asked, "Why doesn't she just stay with you guys?"

"She's worried Mom and Mr. Macartney won't want her. We're done in here," I said, wiping my forehead on my sleeve. "Let's do the bedrooms now."

As we climbed the stairs, Mona asked, "You think maybe you'll work up to calling Mr. Macartney something other than Mr. Macartney by the time they get married, Ab?"

I pretended not to hear as I pushed ahead of her, saying, "You take the room down the hall; I'll do the master bedroom."

"Okay, Abbey, but I hope you're calling him something else by the time they walk down the aisle. Maybe you should talk to him about your cousin."

"I can't hear you!" I called from the master bedroom. "Now get to work!"

"I'll bet if you confided in him, called him by his first name, he'd say he'd be delighted if Katherine stayed. I'll bet—"

"Am I crazy, or am I the only one here washing windows, sports fans?" I yelled, making her laugh.

The last thing Mona said before we parted that afternoon was, "I think you should talk to Kevin Macartney about your cousin, Abbey. Seriously."

"But I hardly know him."

"Maybe it's time you got to know him."

"What's the rush?" I asked, forcing a laugh. "They haven't even set their wedding date. I've got plenty of time."

As soon as I turned the car into the driveway, I heard the roar of a motorcycle coming down Silverwood Road. Don't tell me, I thought, looking in the rearview mirror. A moment later, Rick Risteen—with Katherine riding behind, her arms wrapped around his waist—zipped into the driveway behind me. As I pulled up in front of the house, he let her off the bike. I waited until he'd roared back down the driveway.

Then I turned to my cousin. "How many times do we have to tell you?"

She shrugged. "I know about your rule, but he offered me a ride home, and Mrs. Costello didn't care what I did."

"*We* care, Katherine. Do you deliberately break rules? Do you want me to tattle to Mom on you?" I asked as we went up the steps.

"No. I won't do it again, Abbey. This time I promise." The way she smiled at me, I couldn't help but smile back. Katherine was so pretty. With that short dark hair and those big hazel eyes, she was positively angelic-looking. Besides, I figured a promise was a promise.

A few hours later, I was stretched out in the window seat, preparing to pick up where I'd left off in *Great Expectations*. I sighed contentedly, luxuriating in the knowledge that everyone was going to be out tonight. It would be the first night since Katherine had arrived that I was going to have the house to myself. Mom was going out with her fiancé, Joyce was going to a friend's house, and Shel was taking Katherine to a party given by one of his Fitchett Academy friends.

I opened my book and began to read. Soon, I was right there in the skiff with Pip, gliding swiftly down the Thames, helping Magwitch, the convict and Pip's benefactor, escape. My heart began pounding as another skiff appeared out of nowhere and went after them. Suddenly—

My twin burst into the room. "Emergency! Emergency! You've got to come with us tonight, Ab!"

"Wrong. I don't *have* to do anything tonight, Sheldon."

"Oh, yes, you do. Katherine says she won't go to this party with Don Champion unless *you* come, too."

"So? She's only thirteen. She shouldn't be going

out with that Don Juan anyway. Hey, quite a good pun. Did you get it? Don the Don Juan?" I laughed.

"Yeah, sure, Ab. Listen, Don said he'd fix me up with Hilary Ann Deets if I fixed him up with Katherine, so you have to—"

"You've got a date with someone named *Deets*? Where do you find these people?" I burst into more merry peals, until he yanked me out of the window seat.

Pushing his face into mine, he snapped, "Hilary Ann Deets is one sweet tomato. Now, you'll want to jazz yourself up a bit, Ab." He started pulling me toward the closet.

But I dug in my heels, saying, "Allow me to repeat that I am *not* going out tonight."

"Are, too," said he. I stuck out my chin and crossed my arms. The next thing I knew, he'd picked me up. By the time he put me down in front of the closet, we were both giggling. "You've got to go, Ab. If you don't care about me, think of poor little Katherine. Look how quiet and sad she's been lately. Maybe meeting some new people will cheer her up."

I opened my mouth to protest . . . and bit my lip. He might be right. I was just about to say so when he grinned and clapped me on the back, crying, "I knew you'd see it my way, Ab. Now hurry up and get dressed." Whistling, he left the room.

That's how I ended up crammed into the backseat of Don Champion's car along with Sheldon and his date, Hilary Ann Deets. Wouldn't you know Hilary

Ann was the type who giggled every time my twin opened his mouth, which (as those of us who knew him were aware) was all too often?

Nothing like being a fifth wheel, I thought darkly, staring at the back of my cousin's sleek head. Brother, what an operator she turned out to be. She'd waited until thirty minutes before Don was due to pick her and Shel up to announce she wasn't going unless I came, too. What else could I do but agree to go?

Just call me Abbey the family peacemaker, sports fans.

Sheldon elbowed me. "You keep sighing. What's the problem?"

"Why, not a thing!" I gave him a giant fake smile. "Everything's peachy."

"This party's going to be a blast and a half," said Don. "You'll be glad you came along, Abigail."

I sighed again. Don never could get my name right. As he slipped an arm around my cousin, Shel and Hilary Ann started snuggling.

And a hollow voice inside asked, Are we having fun yet?

A few minutes later, good old Sheldon piped up, "Don't worry about Bassett Hunter tonight, either, Ab. I told him I'd mutilate him if he put the moves on you again."

"You didn't!" I gasped.

"No kidding?" Don started laughing. "The Bassett's after your sister, eh, Shel?"

Good thing he turned into a driveway and stopped the car just then, because I had my hand on the door handle, preparing to leap out rather than bear this humiliation any longer.

As our merry band trooped up the driveway, Katherine turned to me and said, "Oh, Abbey, remind me that I want to talk to you about that wonderful story you wrote."

"*Abbey* wrote a wonderful story?" Guess Who repeated.

"I thought I'd hidden it in my drawer," I said pointedly.

"No," said Katherine. "You left it right on top of the bureau, so I thought you wouldn't mind if I read it. I really liked it."

Hilary Ann quit making googly eyes at my twin long enough to ask, "What's it about?"

"Nothing much," I answered, fast. "Just a little something I dashed off. I won't bore you with the—"

Sheldon clapped me on the back, crying, "Can the false modesty and tell us about it, for crying out loud!"

"It's just a humorous little thing I jotted down," I mumbled, turning bright red. "I don't want to talk about it, guys, really."

"Nonsense," said Katherine, laughing. "It's a very funny story. I'm sure it'll be accepted by your school's magazine, Abbey."

"Well, I would *hope* so," Shel crowed. "She's the short-story editor, after all."

"Oh, well," Hilary Ann said knowingly.

"Yeah, it's in the bag," Don agreed, sounding bored as he opened the front door for Katherine.

Did she drop the subject? Did she just go inside and join the party, leaving me whatever dignity I had left? She did not. She said, "Wait until you read it, Shel. It's about unrequited love, but it's not a hackneyed romance. The girl in Abbey's story is mentally deranged and—"

I forced a laugh, saying, "That's enough, Katherine. Really . . ."

"It's so amusing!" she went on. "This strange girl murders the boy she loves because he doesn't love her back." She burst out laughing.

There was a pause while everyone stared at me. "Sounds like a laugh a minute," Shel deadpanned. Hilary Ann burst into a torrent of giggles.

Giving Shel a dazzling fake smile, I said, "As a matter of fact, I patterned the boy in my story after *you.*"

Hilary Ann stopped giggling and shot me a look. As she and my twin walked away, Don and Katherine disappeared into the living room . . . and there I was, alone again.

I smiled idiotically at the mob of total strangers swirling around me, thinking, If I can just make it through the next hour or so, I can probably find someone to take me home.

I noticed a tall, thin boy with carroty hair staring at me from across the hall. He smiled and started toward me. Maybe this won't be so bad, I thought. Who knows? I might even meet a new and interesting person tonight.

Wrong-o.

Bassett Hunter whipped out of the living room, cutting off the tall, thin stranger. "Abbey!" he cried, throwing his arms around me. "Don just told me you were here!"

My mother's advice rang in my ears: Be nice without encouraging him. So as soon as he released me, I tried for a "nice" smile that wouldn't encourage him. "How've you been, Bassett?" I asked in a neutral tone.

His pale-blue eyes fairly glowed with warmth as he answered in a deeply sincere voice, "Wonderful now that you're here."

Oh, Lord. Bassett was the nicest person in the world; he really was. He was sort of cute, with short, curly brown hair, an open honest face, and soulful blue eyes that shone behind the thick lenses of his glasses. He had the smile of an angel.

So it freaked me out that he kissed like a sex maniac. It just goes to prove you can't judge a book by its cover. If I were to compare the way Bassett looked to a book, I would say he looked like a good wholesome classic like *Swiss Family Robinson.* Meanwhile, he kissed like *Peyton Place.*

"Can I get you a Coke or 7UP, Abbey?"

I looked around. Shel and Hilary Ann weren't in sight. Katherine was at the far end of the living room, surrounded by a group of admiring boys. I was on my own, sports fans. Mustering a smile, I said, "7UP would be great; thanks."

He grabbed my hand. "Come on downstairs. The party's much better down there. I'm so glad you came. You've made my night, Abbey."

The basement room was dark and crowded with dancing couples. We made our way toward a table covered with soda cans and bowls of chips. Bassett popped the top of a can of 7UP and handed it to me. I took a sip and glanced around just as Shel and Hilary Ann entered the room.

Uh-oh, I thought. It looked as if Shel was going to dance. What he lacked in coordination, he made up for in enthusiasm. My twin usually cleared the floor, as a matter of fact. When Shel danced, people *watched*—with incredulous expressions on their faces.

A drippy Barry Manilow number started playing, and Shel draped himself over Hilary Ann.

"I'm crazy about this song," a deep voice murmured in my ear. I looked up into Bassett's soulful eyes. Holding out his arms, he commanded, "Dance with me."

He looked so happy, I didn't have the heart to say no. So I put down my soda and danced. And what do you know? Bassett knew how. We did a graceful box step around the room, and I realized I was enjoying myself.

I noticed my cousin standing with Don across the room. As I watched, a tall, dark guy walked up to them. He had his back to me, so I couldn't see his face, but I noticed he had something tucked under his arm. He also seemed to be talking only to Katherine, who smiled and nodded while old Don looked more and more sour. Then the other guy handed Katherine what looked like a can of beer. He gave one to Don, too.

"You're frowning," Bassett pointed out. "Did I step on your foot? I'm really sorry; I didn't mean to. That is so gauche."

"You didn't step on me. You're a good dancer, Bassett."

"That's what I love about you," he said in his deeply sincere way. "You're a very kind person, Abbey." He smiled, and I found myself smiling back.

Error. He pulled me tight against him, whispering into my ear, "I'm mad for you!"

Good grief, I thought, here we go again.

Luckily, just at that moment, good old Sheldon danced by with Hilary Ann. For once in my life, my twin was a welcome interference. He stuck an elbow between me and Bassett, saying, "Watch it, Hunter," in such a way that poor Bassett released me like a hot potato.

"Excuse me." It was the tall, thin redhead I'd noticed earlier. "You don't mind if I cut in, do you?" Without waiting for a reply, he whisked me away from Bassett, who gazed sadly after us. "I'm Bill Whipple," the redhead said. "You're Shel Reilly's sister, right?"

I had just noticed Katherine again. She put her beer can down on the table behind her. My mouth dropped open as the dark-haired guy handed her another one. "You're not Shel's sister?" Bill asked. "I thought—"

"No, I mean, yes, I am. I'm not frowning at you. It's my cousin over there . . . have you met her? Come on." Without waiting for his reply, I took off toward Katherine and Don.

"*Ça va!*" my cousin greeted me.

"Hey there, Abbey," a deep voice said. I turned to see none other than Rick Risteen. "Like a beer?"

"No, thank you. What are you doing here anyway?" I asked.

"He's a crasher," Don snapped, glaring at Rick.

"I'm a friend of a friend of a friend," Rick corrected him, and grinned at Katherine, who ignored both of them. She was too busy tipping the beer to her lips.

"Want to go to the bathroom with me?" I asked. Without waiting for her reply, I took the beer out of her hand, put it on the table, and took her by the arm. "This way." We were halfway up the stairs before she started to struggle.

After some searching, I located the bathroom in the back hall. I pulled Katherine inside and locked the door. Propping my hands up on my hips, I faced her. "What do you think you're doing?"

"*Qu'est-ce que c'est?*" she asked, and sat down abruptly on the toilet. Fortunately, the lid was down.

"Speak English, Katherine. What do you think you're doing, drinking at your age?"

She stared at me for a moment. Then she slapped a hand over her mouth, giggling. I had to grab her to keep her from slipping off the toilet. Suddenly she paled, gasping, "Oh, I don't feel good."

"I wouldn't feel good if I'd chugged two beers either! I wanted to go home early, but obviously I can't now, and all because of you."

She clutched her stomach, squinting up at me. "How come?"

"You're drunk. Not only can you not go home like this, but I can't leave you here with that barracuda Rick Risteen." I sniffed, adding, "Not to mention Don Juan. Come on, let's find the kitchen and I'll make you some coffee."

I took her hand and tried to pull her to her feet, but she held on to the toilet with her free hand. "I'm not drunk, just relaxed, *ma chère*. Very, very relaxed."

"I'll say," I snapped, steadying her as she started to slip off the toilet seat again. "You can't even *sit* straight."

"I don't want to leave," she protested weepily as I unlocked the door. "I'm just having fun. You don't think I should do anything, Abbey. You just want me to sit at home like you do and read poetry all the time!" Her voice rose as I led her out into the hall and pulled her toward the kitchen.

"Sh!" I hissed. "Calm down, will you. Look, I know that Don Champion. I went out with him last spring."

"So?" she said, and hiccuped.

"He thinks he's God's gift to women." I pulled a chair out from the table and gently pushed her into it.

"He's not smart enough to be God's gift to women," she said, giggling and wobbling around in the chair. "Anyway, I don't care. . . . I like him and I want to go back to the—"

I pushed her back down, saying, "You're not going anywhere except home."

"Home?" she said in a small voice. "I don't have a . . . home."

I figured now was not the time to argue with her and continued rummaging around until I found a jar of instant coffee. After filling the kettle on the stove with water, I spooned some coffee into a cup. Fortunately, Katherine seemed to have calmed down a bit. In fact, she'd put her head down on her arms. Good grief, maybe she's passed out, I thought.

I decided I'd better find Shel and ask him to get us a ride home right away. If everything went according to plan, I could easily get Katherine home and into bed before Mom got home from her date.

Later, when I thought back on it, I was amazed that I had believed that anything ever went according to plan.

Seventeen

Apparently, the minute I left Katherine to go back downstairs to find my twin, she headed outside, where she met Rick Risteen and his friends, who had beer and who knows what else. At any rate, they were having their own party out there under the stars.

I finally found Shel talking to a bunch of people and I explained about Katherine. By the time he explained to Hilary Ann about having to leave her on her own for a little bit, that he'd be back for her, Don Champion had gotten on his high horse, not to mention that he was mad as a hornet at Rick for getting Katherine drunk. He followed me and Shel back upstairs, loudly declaring that if anyone was going to take Katherine home, he was, etc., etc.

"She's gone," I said, staring into the empty kitchen. The teakettle was steaming, so I quickly turned off the burner. Then I looked at my twin and Don. "We'd better spread out. One of you look upstairs, one down." I sighed as Don whirled around and crashed smack into Shel. "Don, you search this floor; Shel, you look upstairs. I'll check the bathroom."

After making sure Katherine wasn't in the bathroom, I decided to check the kitchen again. But then
I heard a commotion. People were shouting and running up the basement stairs. As I ran into the front
hall, Shel came out of the living room and Don bar-
reled down from upstairs. "Bassett!" I called as he
came up from the basement. "What's going on?"

"Someone said there's a fight outside."

Shel and I looked at each other and headed for the
front door. We didn't have to exchange a word to
know that Katherine was probably right in the middle of it.

A bunch of guys were wrestling around on the
grass. Two were arm-wrestling, the others were basically just horsing around. Kids stood around in
clumps, talking and laughing. "It's nothing serious,"
I said, relieved.

"Oh, brother," Shel groaned, and pointed toward
the turnaround.

"Katherine!" I hollered. "Don't you dare!" She
was trying to hop onto the back of Rick Risteen's
motorcycle, but she had had so much beer that her
coordination was off. A big burly blond boy stood
next to her, laughing. Rick grinned and said something, which was lost in the roar of his bike. He
gunned the motor as Katherine staggered backward
slightly and tried again.

Shel put his mouth close to my ear, asking, "What
do you think we should do?"

Before I could answer, Don Champion bounded

down the front steps toward Katherine, hollering something.

Rick saw him coming and switched off the motor. All the laughter and chatter stopped as he got off the motorcycle. One of his friends held it as he walked over to Don. "She was just going to take a spin around the block," he said. "There's no harm in that, is there?"

"She happens to be with me," said Don. A few of Rick's friends puffed out their chests and moved in closer. Don turned to Katherine. "Tell him," he said. "Tell him you're with me."

She giggled and shrugged as Don grabbed her hand.

The biggest of Rick's friends walked stiff-legged up to Don. "Problem, buddy?" he asked.

"Now, now," Bassett began, "there's no reason for—"

"The young lady is my date," said Don. "So the rest of you can just butt out." Rick and his friends looked at each other and burst into raucous laughter. I felt sorry for Don, I swear. He acted like a doofus sometimes, but still . . .

I followed Shel down the steps. He was a midget compared to Rick's friends. Even so, he went over and stood by Don while I went over to Katherine.

"I'll drive you home, Katherine," said Don. "That's final."

"I'm just going for a ride. I'll be right back," she told him.

141

"Not on a motorcycle, you won't," I said, and collared her.

"Let go!" She pulled away, trying to break my grip on her arm, but I held on. I hadn't spent years defending myself against Sheldon for nothing, boy. Katherine didn't have a chance against me.

And Don didn't have a chance against Rick Risteen and his pals either. "Get lost, fella," one of them told Don, and shoved him.

"Leave her alone, Abbey," said Rick. "She's a big girl."

"Don't hurt him!" Katherine cried. It wasn't clear which guy she was worried about. All I know is that when Don lunged, Rick wheeled around with his fist out. Don went down like a rock, sports fans.

"I can't believe this," I whispered to Shel. "Every time I see Don, he starts a fight."

"At least he finished it this time," Shel muttered. "That's enough," he told Rick. Then he and Bassett helped Don to his feet.

"I don't feel so . . . good," Katherine gasped, hanging on to me. "I want to go home now."

"You're something," I told her. "Just a while ago you accused me of being a killjoy. Now that you've started a rumble, you want to go home. You ought to be ashamed of yourself," I lectured as I led her down the driveway to Don's car. "Not only are you way too young to drink, but look at poor Don. Are you okay, Don?" I called over my shoulder.

"My node . . . I thing id's brogen."

When we reached the car, Bassett helped Don into the passenger side, saying he'd drive. Katherine started to get into the backseat. Suddenly, she gasped and bolted out again.

Just in time, too, I thought, as she threw up all over the yard.

The next morning, Katherine was green. "Why did you let me drink beer?" she had the unmitigated gall to whine. "I feel *awful*." She pulled the sheet up to her chin and closed her eyes.

"You've got a nerve," I said. "I didn't exactly pour it down your throat, you know."

Joyce put her head around the door. "Mom wants to know if Katherine's all right, Abbey. She also said to tell you she wants to have a talk with you."

I sighed. "You mean she wants to lecture me for a change. Come on, Katherine, get up. I'm not facing this alone."

"The last time I got up, I vomited."

"Then stay where you are!" said Joyce. "Ab, you better get down there. Mom's pretty upset."

Katherine opened one eye, saw me glaring at her, and groaned, closing it again. "I hope you realize," I hissed, "that the only reason I haven't dragged you out of bed by your *hair* is because you're so sick." Then I turned and stomped out of the room.

A few minutes later, I was slouched on the couch across from my mother in the wing chair. She had her I-can't-believe-you've-let-me-down look on her face. "Mom, there was nothing I could do."

"But I depend on you to keep an eye on her," Mom said. "You obviously lost track of her last night. She's much too young to experiment with beer."

"Mom, I tried, I honestly did. But Katherine's a handful—face it. Boys just flock to her!" I waved my arms around. "College boys! Who do you think gave her all the beer?"

Whoops, I thought as my mother sat up straight.

"What do you mean, college . . . ? I thought she went to a party at one of Shel's friends'. . . . Oh, Abbey, I am very disappointed in you."

You let her go out with Rick Risteen, I thought indignantly. Meanwhile, I hung my head, trying to look contrite. Great, I thought as Sheldon wandered into the room. The golden boy was just what I needed at this point.

"What's going on?" he asked between chomps on the apple he was eating.

"We're discussing what happened last night," Mom answered.

Shel came around the chair and peered into my face. I gave him a look that should have killed, and what did he do? He raised one blond eyebrow, asking, "Troubles, bubbles?"

"Shut *up!*" I shouted.

"You two stop it right now," Mom ordered. "I am very distressed. Katherine is our responsibility, and I'm concerned about her."

"I tried to control her," I said. "But, I mean, she's got free will. I'm not her keeper."

"But, Abbey, you're older than she is and . . . oh, dear." She shook her head. "Maybe this is just too much for all of us right now. I know I'm asking a lot of you kids. You have to adjust to my remarriage and—"

"We can handle it, Mom," Shel said, frowning at me.

"Whaddya mean, *we*?" I demanded. "I don't see you doing much about Katherine!"

"The trouble is," Mom went on, ignoring Sheldon and me, "she really doesn't have anyplace else to go at this point."

"She's got Aunt Claudia, doesn't she?" Shel asked, sounding surprised.

Mom glanced at the doorway. In a low voice, she said, "Claudia told me before she left that the man she's marrying doesn't want the responsibility of a teenage stepdaughter."

What a nerve, I thought, and bit my tongue.

"Obviously, that is not something Katherine needs to know," Mom went on.

"She can stay with us, can't she?" I asked.

"I haven't discussed it with Kevin yet. Until I do, I'd rather you two not say a word to Katherine."

"We won't; don't worry, Mom," Shel said.

She looked so upset that I took a deep breath and said, "I'll make sure she stays out of trouble from now on, Mom."

"Even if trouble's her middle name with a capital *T,* right, Ab?" Shel asked.

"It's not a joking matter, Sheldon."

"Aw, lighten up!" He ruffled my hair, adding, "I'm just adding a little levity to the—*oof!*" he said as I socked him in the stomach. "Did you see that, Ma? Did you *see* what she did to me?"

"Yes, I did," Mom said, calmly. Turning back to me, she added, "You promise me, Abbey, you'll make sure we don't have a repeat of last night?"

"I promise." Then I grinned and nodded at Sheldon, who was hamming it up, staggering around the room with his tongue hanging out of his mouth. Mom shook her head, pressing her lips together to keep from smiling.

Finally, Sheldon canned the histrionics and threw himself onto the couch beside me. "Now that Abbey's decided to grow up and accept her responsibility for Katherine," he said innocently, "let's discuss Aunt Claudia for a moment, Ma. What kind of a person is she? I mean, if you ask me, she's not too stable."

"Who asked you?" I asked, and mimed cracking up.

Mom gave me a look. I shut up. Turning back to Shel, she said, "My sister is not like most people, that's certain. She never has been. I will tell you truthfully that I don't . . . like her very much."

"You don't like your own *sister?*" I asked. "Mom, that's sad."

She nodded. "It really is. But it happens in the best of families. You know, kids, it makes me happy, seeing Katherine with you three this summer. I think it's good for her to be part of a happy family, to see how you all get along."

"Or *don't* get along," I said, shooting a look at Sheldon.

"You do, though," she insisted. "You three rough-house a lot, but basically you look after each other."

I sniffed. "Yeah, only the looking-after frequently borders on harassment, not to mention torture."

Sheldon widened his eyes. "How can you *say* such a thing, Ab?"

"That's what a family is all about," Mom said. "You kids challenge each other. I think it teaches you something about coping with life. Katherine's never had to deal with brothers and sisters, but she has dealt with not knowing her father and having a mother who isn't around very much. What do you think her life has been like?"

Shel and I looked at each other, wide-eyed. "No wonder she says she likes it here," I finally said.

"That's why I'm asking you to make room for her," Mom went on, "even though it's not always easy. Abbey, go up and ask her if she wants some soup, please. She hasn't eaten anything all day."

Eighteen

The next Saturday, Shel and I drove over to visit Gram. Or rather, I drove because I had hidden the keys and wouldn't produce them until he agreed it was my turn.

As I turned off at the Greenwich exit, I glanced at him. "You're frowning," I pointed out. "I drive just as well as you do, Sheldon."

"I was thinking about Katherine, Ab. Maybe she learned something after that party. She's been good as gold lately, have you noticed?"

"Too good, if you ask me. I have a funny feeling that she's up to something."

"Man, oh, man, you're never satisfied. When she first came, you complained about her tagging along with you all the time. Then you were jealous when she stole Rick Risteen away from you—"

"She didn't steal anyone away from me," I snapped. "Rick Risteen may *look* good, but he has the personality of a pea."

For a split second I thought I'd had the last word.

Then he laughed, saying, "Don't tell me the little coconut is growing up!"

"For your information, my hair is growing out, Sheldon."

"Yeah, I've noticed." He leaned across the seat to peer at me. "You stopped combing it with a toothbrush yet, Ab?"

Even though I wanted to choke him, I had to laugh.

As I turned onto Gram's road, he said, "Seriously, I don't think Katherine can do anything right, as far as you're concerned. Why don't you give her a break?"

"But I sense she's up to something. For one thing, she doesn't talk to me anymore."

"So, do something about it, Ab."

"Like what?"

"I don't know." He shrugged. "What would you do if Joyce quit talking to you?"

"I'd keep after her," I answered. "But I can't bug Katherine like that."

"Why not?"

"She'd hate me for it," I answered.

"So what?" he said as I pulled into the driveway. "If you're really worried about Katherine, maybe you should risk that, Ab." As we got out of the car, he said, "Hey, you know, you're *not* a bad driver."

Suddenly I thought of an expression Dad always used. "Praise from Sir Hubert is praise indeed!" I yelled, and clapped him on the back before taking off for the house.

Gram opened the door just as he caught up to me. "Hi, there!" he said, dropping his hands from around my neck.

"Come in, darlings," she said, laughing. I couldn't

tell if she was amused because she'd caught Sheldon being his usual obnoxious self, or if she was just glad to see us. This was one of the things I loved most about Gram—whenever I visited, she acted as if I'd made her day.

After getting glasses of iced tea, the three of us went out to sit on the terrace overlooking Long Island Sound. Once she was settled in a chaise longue, Gram said, "Well, tell me all about your mother's wedding plans."

Shel slid his eyes at me, saying, "She hasn't really done anything about it yet."

"They haven't even set a date," I explained.

"I must say, your mother is like a new woman," she said. "It's wonderful. . . ." She looked out over the sparkling water. Her blue eyes had that faraway look that told me she was thinking of Dad, her only child.

Late that afternoon, I went running with Mona and Crystal. As we jogged along, Mona asked, "Has Abbey told you about her mother's plans, Crystal?"

"No. What are they?" Crystal asked.

"She's marrying Kevin Macartney," I said.

"I know him. That's great," Crystal said as if she meant it. Then, "Does this mean you're going to move, Abbey?"

"I never even considered that," Mona said. "I'd *die*, Ab."

"Yes; our track team needs you," said Crystal.

Their reactions were so characteristic, I had to

smile. "Don't worry," I told them as we jogged up River Road. "My mother says they're looking for a house in this school system."

"Oh, good," Mona said. "Let's walk for a while, you guys." As we slowed to a walk, she asked, "So, when's the wedding, Ab?"

"Not for a long time," I answered confidently. "They're in no hurry. They want to have a house before they set the date."

"How big a house are they looking for?" Crystal asked, pulling the rubber band out of her ponytail so that her amber mane spilled over her shoulders.

I ran my hand over my longish stubble and stifled a sigh, answering, "Mom says Mr. Macartney wants a house with enough bedrooms for all of us, plus a guest room."

Crystal arched an eyebrow. "Honestly, Abbey, don't you think it's time you called him by his first name?"

"Have you two been discussing this?" I snapped. "Sorry, guys. . . . It's just that all the *ifs* freak me out."

"What *ifs?*" Mona asked gently.

"What if Mr. Macartney hates Joyce and Shel and me? What if Mom forgets about us?" I dropped my eyes. "Don't tell me I sound like a four-year-old. . . . I know it, but I can't help it."

"We'd never tell you that," Mona soothed. "Don't worry. It's going to be great."

This was one of the drawbacks to telling people, even a good friend like Mona, your most secret fears.

Too often, people tried to cheer you up by telling you not to worry. Easier said than done, sports fans. All I really wanted my friends to say was, "I understand."

That was why when I got home and discovered Katherine in the window seat, crying, and she refused to talk about it, I didn't bug her. Especially when she said, "Please try to understand; it's something only I can solve."

So all I did was squeeze her hand and ask, "Would talking to Mom help?"

She shook her head, trying to smile. She looked about six years old with her eyes red from crying and her usually perfect complexion all blotchy. "I'm afraid to talk to Aunt Evelyn, Abbey. She might get angry at Claudia."

I considered telling her that family members get mad at each other all the time; what was the big deal? But then I decided it was none of my business. She was entitled to privacy, wasn't she? So I kept my mouth shut.

I kept my mouth shut later that night, too, when I found her in Mom's room, talking on the phone. From the way she hung up as soon as I walked in, I knew something was up. But what?

The next day was Monday, the beginning of my last week baby-sitting for the Costello kids at their club. That afternoon, I found out that Katherine was definitely planning something. And it was none other than Rick Risteen who told me.

The kids and I were in the baby pool when a voice called, "Yo!"

I looked over my shoulder and spotted Rick on the other side of the chain-link fence. I hadn't spoken to him since the night of the party. "Are you addressing me?" I asked.

"Who else? Do me a favor and tell your cousin my bike will be back from the garage by Saturday." Then he turned and strolled away.

She wouldn't dare, I thought. Just wait until I get home this afternoon. I'll confront her with Rick's message and demand an explanation just like I would if she were Joyce.

I bit my lip. But Katherine wasn't Joyce. And if I did make a big deal out of Rick's message, wouldn't she just accuse me of being jealous again?

I was overjoyed to find Mom bustling around the kitchen when I got home late that afternoon. "It's a miracle!" I cried. "You're home early. Don't tell me something's wrong at the office . . . ?"

"Don't be so apprehensive." She laughed as she got spaghetti and tomato sauce out of a cupboard. "Everything's fine at the office, Abbey. That's why I'm home early."

As she filled a pot with water, I said, "Well, I'm glad, Ma, because I need to talk to you about—"

"There's something I need to discuss with *you*," she interrupted. "Sit down."

Her tone made the hair on the back of my head rise. I forgot all about Katherine as we sat down at the kitchen table. "Didn't Kevin do a nice job repairing this?" she asked, running her hand over the tabletop. Her smile faded. "I wanted to talk to you before the other kids, Abbey."

I forced a laugh. "You mean to say I've beaten out the competition?" Meanwhile, I was thinking, Now what?

In a breathless voice, my mother said, "Kevin wants me to go to Massachusetts with him this weekend to meet some old friends." She looked at me expectantly.

When she didn't say anything more, I prompted, "And . . . ?"

She sat back. "I thought you'd be upset."

"Because you're going away with my stepfather-to-be?" I asked, and winced, making her smile faintly. "Gosh, that sounds weird. Do you think I'll ever feel comfortable calling Mr. Macartney Kevin, Ma?"

"I'm sure you will, dear. Just give it time."

"Because, really, calling my mother's husband Mr. Macartney isn't too swift. Although I guess I've got plenty of time to get used to it before you two tie the knot, right? So, when are you leaving for the weekend?"

"After work on Friday. We'll be home Sunday night. I wanted to talk to you first, thinking you might help me tell Shel and Joyce."

"Mom, forgive me for being dense, but since when have you needed my help telling them you're going away for the weekend?"

"I . . . we're not *married* yet, and we'd be staying at a motel together." She put a hand over her heart, adding, "I dread telling your grandmother about this."

"Mom . . ." I shook my head, fighting the impulse to laugh; at the same time, I could feel the prickle of tears in my eyes. "I don't think Gram will think anything of it."

"But what about your brother and sister? Joyce is only eleven and your brother has been the man of the house since your father died. . . . Oh, dear . . ." Her voice trailed off as her eyes filled with tears. "Now I wish I'd told Kevin this isn't a good idea. I just can't leave the three of you."

"The four of us," I reminded her.

"Yes." She stood up. "I'm going to call him to tell him it won't work."

"Mother," I said firmly, "put that phone down. I'm positive Joyce and Sheldon will take this in stride. Look how *I'm* taking it. Usually *I'm* the one who blows things out of proportion, right? Plus, it'd be fun to be left on our own for the weekend. You know you can *trust* us, don't you?"

She hung up the phone. "Of course I do, Abbey. I must say, you seem very adult all of a sudden."

I laughed modestly. "Face it: I *am* an adult. I'm sixteen, after all. Besides, you and Mr. Macartney are engaged to be married. It's not as if you're just having a meaningless fling!"

She turned pink. "That's . . . another thing I

wanted to talk to you about," she said.

I gasped. "You *are* having a meaningless fling?"

She closed her eyes and started laughing weakly. "No, dear. . . . Kevin and I have set our wedding date."

So much for the newly wise and grown-up Abbey Reilly, brother. I went absolutely cold inside. *"When?"*

"The first Saturday in December. We decided not to put it off to the new year. We've decided where to live, too."

I swear I felt faint. Gripping the edge of the kitchen table, I said, "I'm going to have a catatonic fit if you say we're leaving Norwalk!"

She smiled. "Relax. We're going to exercise my option to buy this house. Eventually we'll put on an addition."

"I can't believe it!" I yelled, leaping out of my chair. "It's a miracle! *Something's going to stay the same!* I'm saved!" My mother broke up as I started rock and rolling around the kitchen.

Nineteen

Mom and Mr. Macartney couldn't have reached the end of the driveway on Friday night before Shel was rubbing his hands together, chortling, "Man, this is going to be a blast! Do you girls realize we are *free?* We can do anything we want this weekend!"

"Nunh, unh," said Joyce. "You promised Mom there'd be no monkey business, Sheldon."

His face fell. "Oh, yeah. Man, what a drag. We've got a house to ourselves, but we have to act responsible. Life is definitely unfair."

Joyce and I laughed, but Katherine just went on picking at her goulash. I was trying to think of something to say to include her in the conversation when the phone rang.

Shel and Joyce jumped up, leaving me no choice but to join the stampede. Naturally, Sheldon cheated by grabbing Joyce's and my shirttails and whipping us away from the phone.

"Hel-lo?" he said in his best macho-man voice. "Yeah, hold on." He dropped the receiver, which hit the floor with a crash. "For you, Ab."

I picked up the phone, and a familiar voice said, "I take it that was your brother."

"*Packy!* How *are* you? How come you never wrote? When did you get home?"

"This afternoon. I missed you," he said warmly.

"I bet." I laughed. "That's why I got so many letters from you, right? It's so good to hear from you, Pack."

"How'd you like to go out tonight, Ab? I've got the car, and a bunch of kids are going to meet over at Crystal's house, maybe go out for something to eat later. How about it?"

"Sounds like fun. Uh, is it okay if my cousin comes, too? She's living here for the summer."

"Sure. I'll pick you up in half an hour," he said, and hung up.

I turned to find everyone looking at me. Joyce propped her hands up on her hips, saying, "If everyone goes out tonight, I'll be alone."

"And don't even think about taking the car, dog face. I claimed first dibs before supper."

"I don't need the car, smarty pants, and stop calling me dog face. As for you," I said, stroking Joyce's wispy blond hair, "couldn't you manage a couple of hours alone so that Katherine and I can go up to Crystal's? We'd be home by eleven or so."

She poked her little lip out, but then Katherine said, quietly, "If you don't mind, I'd rather not go. I'll stay with Joyce."

"Thanks, Katherine," said Joyce. Shooting me a look, she added, "I'm glad *someone* around here cares about me."

"Hey!" I protested. "You make it sound as if I don't give you the time of day, Joyce. Who wrote the sales pitch for your five hundred boxes of greeting cards?"

Meanwhile, Shel was saying, "Good thing we've got Katherine, huh, Joyce?" It was the first time I'd heard Katherine laugh since the party fiasco.

As Packy opened the passenger door of his father's car for me, he said, "I'm glad your cousin didn't want to come tonight, Ab."

"So am I, to be truthful. Wait until you meet her, Pack."

"Why?"

"She's beautiful."

"Inside or out?" he asked.

"What do you mean?"

"There's a big difference, Ab." He smiled and closed the door. As he turned the key in the ignition, he said, "I'm glad we're alone because I have to talk to you about something personal. Remember our first date last spring, Abbey?"

Remember it? How could I forget it? "Sure, Pack."

"We've had a lot of fun together, haven't we?"

"We sure have," I said, returning his smile. I studied him in the glow of the streetlights. Packy had pointed elf ears and dark hair that fell straight across his forehead. I'd always loved how his Adam's apple bobbed when he got nervous, like now. . . .

Don't tell me he still wants me to be his girl-friend! We settled that last spring, didn't we?

"I have something important to tell you, Abbey."

"Oh?" Gulp.

"I wanted to tell you before we get to Crystal's."

The next thing I knew, he'd pulled off the road and turned to me.

In a tiny voice, I asked, "What did you want to tell me?"

He swallowed, making his Adam's apple bob again. "You know I consider you one of my best friends. . . ."

"And I think the same way about *you*, Pack. You're one of the neatest guys I've ever . . . and I don't want our relationship to change. I like how uncomplicated just being friends is, you know? I . . ." Ai, yi, yi, I thought as he gave me a loving smile.

"You're such a sweet girl, Abbey."

"I—I feel the same about you, too!"

"You think I'm a sweet girl?" he asked, and broke up.

"No, no—I mean, it's wonderful that you and I can go out just as *friends*. . . ."

His face fell. "Don't tell me you guessed what I wanted to tell you!" he cried.

"Oh, Pack, sixteen is too young to settle down, to get serious about one person. I mean, what do we *know* of life, really?"

"You did guess. Nuts! I wanted to surprise you. I wanted to tell you how wonderful she is, Abbey!"

I stared at him. "She? Who is this *she?*"

In a reverent tone, he answered, "Her name is Beverly. She lives in Cape Elizabeth, Maine. I met her at the camp I worked at."

Jesus, Mary, and Joseph. He's in love with someone else.

Folding his arms on the steering wheel, he rested his chin on them and sighed. "I'm so happy, I can't even believe it; and you guessed, Ab. You know me so well, you'd already figured out I'd fallen in love, hadn't you?"

I managed to shut my mouth. Then I pulled myself together and said, "Of course, and—and I'm very happy for you. *Very.*"

"Thanks, Ab. I knew you would be."

As we walked up Crystal's driveway a few minutes later, Packy slipped his arm through mine, and it was the oddest thing: I felt sad. I felt as if I'd lost something. It was a strange sadness, though. There was a sweetness to it, because I was truly happy for Packy.

"What's Beverly's last name, Pack?"

"Elksnits," he answered. I stopped dead, yanking my arm out of his. "Abbey, what's wrong?"

"I can't believe this . . . I just can't believe this. Beverly doesn't have relatives in Connecticut, does she?"

He nodded eagerly. "She sure does! In fact, I got my summer job through her uncle, Sam Elksnits, who buys a lot of paint from my father. Why, Ab?

Don't tell me you know the Elksnitses."

"Packy." I put my hand on his shoulder. "I am almost *related* to the Elksnitses. Sam Elksnits is married to my almost-stepfather's daughter."

"No kidding? It's got to be the same family, Ab . . . unless there are two Mr. Elksnitses out there with the same first name."

"I really doubt that," I said as we went up the steps.

"You realize what this means, don't you?" he asked as he rang the doorbell.

I looked at him. "What does this mean?"

"If Beverly and I get married, we'll be part of your family. What would you think of that?"

"Hey,"—I shrugged—"my family's growing by leaps and bounds anyway. I can't see the harm in adding a few *friends*." We burst out laughing as Crystal opened the door.

"Don't forget to take off your shoes," she said as we stepped into the hall.

That was one thing about Crystal's house: It was beautiful, with immaculate white wall-to-wall carpeting and millions of expensive-looking knick-knacks everywhere. But it didn't look as if anyone lived there. There were a lot of things in the house, but no signs of life.

"My mother wants us to stay in the family room," Crystal said as we followed her down the hall.

"Where is your mother?" I asked. "I'd like to say hello to her."

She paused, one hand on the cellar door. "She's sitting at the dining room table.... My father's supposed to call tonight."

"I'll be right down. You two go ahead," I said. A moment later, I looked into the dark dining room. "Anybody in here?"

"Who is it?" Mrs. Glass asked. I could just make her out sitting at the end of the table. A match flashed as she lit a cigarette.

"It's Abbey Reilly, Mrs. Glass. How're you?"

"Fine thanks, dear. Turn on the light, will you? It's on the wall to your right." I did, and she said, "That's better." She smiled at me. "Come and talk to me for a while." She patted the chair next to her. As I sat down, she asked, "How is your family?"

"Everyone's great," I said as she exhaled a plume of smoke.

"Crystal says your mother and Kevin Macartney are going to be married. Tell her how happy I am for her, will you?"

"I will," I said, feeling sorry for Mrs. Glass. She was attractive, with dark auburn hair and the same finely chiseled features Crystal had. But there were deep lines on either side of her mouth. And when she smiled, she looked as if she was in pain.

"I guess your mother deserves a bit of happiness after losing your father," she said, stubbing the cigarette out in an overflowing ashtray in front of her. "Do you think people find happiness because they deserve it, Abbey?"

"I don't know," I answered. "Maybe there's as much happiness inside people as there is unhappiness, Mrs. Glass. Maybe we have to decide which one we're going to concentrate on."

"What are you two doing?" someone asked.

I looked around to see Crystal standing in the doorway. "Mother, are you boring Abbey?"

"Crystal," I said, shocked at her tone. "We were talking about something important."

"Thank you, Abbey," Mrs. Glass said, shooting a look at her daughter. "I can see you've been well brought-up."

"Thanks," I said. "I'll tell my mother you said so." As I followed Crystal down to the basement a moment later, I said, "You're awful to your mother."

She threw me a look over her shoulder. "Well, she drives me crazy, the way she just sits there waiting for Dad to call! I tell you . . ." She grabbed my arm, stopping me at the foot of the stairs. "I've learned something from watching my parents, Abbey. I've vowed that I will never sit and wait for a man to call *me,* night after night." She turned away. "She's so unhappy, and . . . it makes me unhappy. Sometimes I wish they'd just get divorced and be done with it."

"Oh, Crystal . . ." I shook my head. "I don't know what to say to you."

"They claim they're staying together for my sake." She pushed her amber-colored hair out of her face, adding, "Sometimes I'd like to tell them they're not doing me any favors."

"Why don't you?"

She turned to me so that I could see the tears in her eyes. "How can I? The responsibility for my mother's broken heart would fall on my shoulders. I don't think I could cope with that, Abbey."

"Then I guess keeping out of it is the best thing you can do. I want you to know I'm sorry for you, Crystal."

She sighed, nodding. "Thanks. I'll tell you one thing: You should thank your lucky stars that your family is so happy, Abbey."

"Who says we're so happy? We fight like fury sometimes, you know. Just as everyone has problems, every family has all sorts of rivalries and petty grievances. Brother," I added, thinking of what a pain Sheldon was, "take it from me—I know whereof I speak!"

She smiled. "I'm sure you do. But tell me something: Wouldn't all of you rather be together than apart?"

"Yeah; I guess."

"Well, I think that's what being a happy family is all about," she said.

I looked at her for a moment before saying, "I never thought of it like that. You're pretty smart, you know that?"

She laughed, saying, "Not so," but I could tell she was pleased. She actually patted me on the shoulder as we walked into the family room.

Twenty

By the time I got downstairs the next morning, Joyce was sitting on a stool with the phone cradled to her ear and a notebook and Mom's address book balanced on her knees.

"Hello, Mrs. Elksnits?" she said as I got the milk carton and an apple out of the fridge. "This is Joyce Reilly, Evelyn's daughter. Hi! Fine; and you? That's good; and your husband? Glad to hear that, Mrs.— you insist I call you Phyllis? Okay, Mrs.—er, Phyllis. I'm calling to ask if you'd like to buy some Gracious Greeting Cards. I've set a goal, you see"—she glared at me as I snorted with sudden laughter—"I'm going to sell five hundred boxes, Mrs.—Phyllis. Would you like to purchase some to help me out?"

After listening for a moment, Joyce said, "Fine; I'll put you down for two boxes." She scribbled something down in the notebook before going on. "Now, how about some for your husband's secretary, Phyllis? It's very convenient not to have to run out to buy a greeting card, you know. Six boxes? Thank you very much! I'll personally deliver them to your door." She hung up the phone and gave me a triumphant smile.

"You are one tough customer," I said admiringly. "I would've let her go after she agreed to buy two boxes."

"She was putty in my hands, Ab. All because you helped me with my sales pitch. I must be getting good at this! Phyllis didn't even get irritated at me like Mom's friend Mrs. Faber did."

I started laughing. "Mrs. Faber got irritated?"

"I'll say. I was afraid she was going to hang up on me. But she ended up taking four boxes, so I guess she wasn't that mad."

"I see a sales career in your future, Joyce. You'll go far."

Turning a page in Mom's address book, she said, "I'd like to talk more, Ab, but I have quite a few calls to make."

"Where's Katherine?" I asked, aiming my apple core at the trash basket.

"I forgot!" she cried, making me miss. The apple core skittered across the kitchen floor. "Katherine must've called Rick Risteen last night, Ab, because he picked her up on his motorcycle early this morning."

I stared at my sister, speechless for a second. Then: "Boy, oh, boy, now I'm mad. Now I'm really, really *mad*."

"I would've woken you up, but I was on the phone with Mrs. Faber, Ab, and Katherine said not to worry. She left you a note on her bunk, she said—"

I didn't hear the rest. I was too busy racing up the

stairs. A moment later, I stormed back into the kitchen, waving Katherine's note. "Read this!" I said, shoving it at Joyce, who read aloud:

Dear Cousins,
    Don't be angry. I am going to New York to meet someone. Don't worry about me. I'll call you soon.

"She's gone too far this time!" I yelled, snatching the note away from her again.

"Don't get so mad," Joyce said tearfully as I paced around the kitchen. "Maybe she went to see her father."

"So what?" I demanded. "Katherine has been warned about motorcycles a hundred times. She just thinks she can get away with this. And Mom trusted us! Not only is Katherine taking advantage, but the rest of us are going to get into trouble. Well, I'm not letting her get away with it this time." I stopped pacing and tried to think.

"Poor Katherine," Joyce said as a tear made its way down her face. "Poor, poor—"

"*Not* poor Katherine! I'm tired of hearing about poor Katherine!" I shouted. "Where's Shel?"

She wiped her eyes. "Still in bed—where else?"

Thank God for that, I thought, racing up the stairs for the second time that morning. Shel will know what to do.

Here's what he said as soon as he was awake enough to understand what I was telling him: "What do you think we should do?"

168

My face fell. "I thought *you'd* know."

"You mean because I have such vast experience with runaway cousins?" He yawned and sat up in bed. "Okay, first thing is, calm down, Ab. Second, think. Do you think we should call Mom?"

I shook my head. "I don't want to bother her just yet. Maybe Katherine will change her mind and . . . just *wait* until I give her a piece of my mind," I said, getting mad again. "We're always tiptoeing around poor little Katherine instead of treating her like we treat each other."

A smile flickered across his face. "Seems to me I tried to point this out to you some time ago," he said.

"Okay, okay, so I get it now, Sheldon. If we care about Katherine, we should treat her the way we treat each other."

"So what do you think we should do?" he asked again.

I looked at Joyce standing in the doorway, watching me, twisting a strand of hair around and around a finger. Turning back to my twin, I asked, "What would we do if Joyce ran away?"

"We'd try to find her," he answered promptly.

"And when we found her," I said, "we'd scream at her, and then we'd ground her for life, at least."

"And *then* we'd tell her how badly she'd scared us," he said.

I thought for a moment, then said, "Okay, let's give Katherine until noon to call. If she hasn't, we'll call Mom."

We spent the next hour wandering around the

house, picking up the phone every five minutes to make sure it was working. When it finally rang, there was no stampede, no horsing around about who would answer it.

Sheldon did. "Hello?" he said calmly, but the muscle twitched in his jaw. Joyce and I clutched each other as we stared at our brother. "Katherine!"

"Thank God," I breathed.

"Where in heck *are* you?" Shel thundered into the phone.

"Don't yell at her!" I whispered. "Or at least find out where she is first."

More calmly, he asked, "Would you mind telling me what's going on?" He listened, frowning intently, not saying anything until I practically lost my mind.

Finally, he said, "Let me get this straight: You and Rick got a flat on the Merritt Parkway. Now he's getting the tire patched and is . . . ? You're determined to go into the city?" He listened for a moment; then: "So that's what this is all about. Katherine, calm down. I'm not saying you shouldn't look up your father. I'm— Okay, I'll hold on." Putting his hand over the receiver, he said, "She's talking to Rick. Apparently she picked this weekend to look up her old man."

"Tell her this is not the way to do it. Tell her to come home right now!" I said.

"Wait . . . yes?" he said into the phone. "There's a lot wrong with the bike besides a flat tire, so you're going to . . . ? *Oh, no you don't!*" he hollered, making Joyce and me jump. Tears started rolling down my little sister's face. "Katherine, you are *not* to hitch into the city!"

"Give me that phone," I ordered, and grabbed it away from him. "Katherine, it's me."

"Oh, Abbey, I'm sorry about this, but—"

"Sorry, my foot! You've got the whole family in an uproar. Joyce is crying because of you, and I haven't seen her cry practically since my father died!"

"I'm sorry," she said again. "Please try to under-stand—"

"Katherine, it's time for *you* to understand. It's fine if you want to talk to your father. But why do it like this? How could you take off without telling us?"

There was silence. Then she said, "I didn't want anyone to know if he didn't want me."

"Oh," I said, suddenly, finally understanding what it must be like to be her. "I see your— Excuse me; Shel's trying to get my attention." I slapped the hand he was waving in my face, asking, *"What?"*

"Why can't we pick her up and drive her into New York right now, Ab?"

I was about to say, "You can't drive in New York City," but he wrestled the phone away from me.

"Stay right where you are, Katherine," he said in his macho-man voice. "We're going to take you into the city personally. That's all right. No, don't cry; it's no trouble at all, honest. We'll be right there."

He hung up and turned to Joyce and me. "Everything's arranged. As usual, the kid has saved the day."

Joyce looked at me . . . and burst into hysterical giggles. I think it was a combination of being upset about Katherine and the ridiculously pleased expression on Shel's face. Whatever—I didn't resist when he took me and Joyce by the arms and marched us out of the house and down to the car.

But when he drove down the driveway at about one hundred miles an hour, I screeched, "If you speed, I'm telling!"

"Me, too," said Joyce. "I don't want to get killed trying to help anyone!"

"Okay, okay," he muttered, braking at the end of the driveway. "Jeez, you two are such warts."

"That's *worry*wart, bozo," I snapped. Joyce burst into nervous giggles again.

Twenty-One

As cars hurtled past us on the East Side Drive, Shel stopped gritting his teeth long enough to ask, "Got your seat belts on, girls?"

"We've got them on," I said. "Just watch the road."

"Man, they drive as if they'd just as soon *kill* you," he muttered.

In the backseat, Katherine said, "I really appreciate this. I'll never forget what you're doing for me."

No one responded. We were too busy holding our breaths as we whipped through a tunnel and out into the light again. We had picked her up twenty minutes earlier at a rest area on the Merritt Parkway. Rick's father was on his way over to pick him up. There had been no conversation to speak of. I think all four of us were too nervous to talk.

As if reading my mind, Shel said, "I'll be glad when this is over."

"You and me both," I agreed. Over my shoulder, I asked, "What was the address again, Katherine?"

"Sixty-ninth Street between First and Second. Do you think I should try to call him first, or just . . . arrive?" she asked.

Shel glanced at me. "What do you think?"

"Call first, I guess," I answered.

There was a pause, then Katherine said, "I'm afraid."

"You shouldn't be," Joyce said. "He's your dad."

"I know, but it might not be a good time. Or . . . or he may be out of town."

Shel sucked in his breath. Then he said, "Do you have any idea if your father still lives at this address, Katherine?"

"N-no," she stammered.

"Don't worry," I said to Shel as much as to our cousin. "Everything's going to turn out fine."

"Abbey always says that," Joyce confided to Katherine as Shel turned off at the Seventy-first Street exit.

"Good job, Shel," I said as we stopped for the traffic light. "That was scary, but you did it."

He wiped his brow, saying, "They don't call me Nerves-of-Steel Reilly for nothing, man."

"Nerves-of-Steel Reilly?" Joyce repeated, and started giggling. She stopped abruptly when the light turned green and Shel hit the gas.

"Whoa!" he said as the car leaped forward. "Sorry about that, girls. My foot slipped."

"I bet," I said. He grinned at me briefly before concentrating on his driving again.

A few minutes later, Katherine said, "Uh, Shel?"

"Don't talk to me now, man. I'm busy."

"But shouldn't we be——?"

"I told you, Ab," he said. "I told you I could handle this. Driving in New York isn't so different from driving anywhere."

"But," said Katherine, "I just saw a sign for Seventy-*fifth* Street."

"So?" he asked, hunched over the steering wheel, his eyes darting from side to side.

"My father lives on Sixty-ninth, which would be *down*town, wouldn't it?"

"She's right," I said. "We're going the wrong way, O Nerves-of-Steel."

"Aw, for . . . why didn't one of you speak up before now? Oh, well, no sweat. I'll just turn around."

And he did—the wrong way onto a one-way street.

"Jeez!" he muttered, furiously turning the wheel and shifting into reverse as the driver of the cab we almost collided with leaned on the horn.

"Hurry up!" Joyce cried, looking out the rear window. "We're making a giant traffic jam!"

He stepped on the gas, and I cringed at the sickening squeal of brakes behind us. "It's okay," Joyce said. "The man's stopped screaming out the window now. He's backing up. . . . Go ahead, Shel. I'll tell you if you're about to hit anything."

Several minutes later, we were headed downtown. "You can come out from under the dashboard now, Abbey," my twin wisecracked. "Man, oh, man, I have to admit I'm looking forward to parking the car and *walking*."

"Just get somewhere near Sixty-ninth and we can," said Katherine. "I'll never forget what you've gone through for me today, Shel."

"What *he's* gone through?" I said. "How about Joyce and me? And you better save your praise until we get there safely, Katherine, because it isn't over yet."

"Oh, yes it is," said Shel, making a ninety-degree left turn onto Sixty-ninth Street.

"You drive like you've lived here all your life, you maniac!" I gasped as he zipped into a parking space so small that only our beat-up subcompact could possibly have made it. He gave me a smug, if shaky, smile and switched off the ignition.

The four of us sat there catching our breaths for a moment. Finally, Shel said, "Well, I guess we'd better get this over with."

We got out of the car. Then we looked at Katherine. Her hazel eyes seemed too big in her pale face. She looked up and down the block, plucking at the waistband of her short orange jumpsuit. Suddenly she looked like the kid she was.

The street Katherine's father lived on was a quiet one. Old brownstones lined one side, apartment buildings lined the other. A few people were out walking their dogs. Midday heat shimmered up from the pavement, although a faint breeze stirred the hair at the nape of my neck.

Katherine sighed, saying, "New York isn't what I expected."

"What did you expect?" I asked.

"More noise and dirt. There are flowers and trees here." She sounded so surprised, I had to smile.

"We've been to New York twice with Mom since we moved to Connecticut," I told her. "But just during the week, when people are rushing in eighteen directions."

"It's much quieter today," Joyce agreed.

"People sleep in on Saturdays," Shel said. "Some of 'em, anyway," he added, shooting a look at Katherine.

"I like New York better on Saturdays," Joyce said. "Want to walk around a little?"

"Sure," I said. Katherine nodded eagerly.

"Hold it!" Shel said as we started to walk up the block.

I turned around. "What? We're just going to—"

"This isn't a pleasure outing," he said, hands on hips. "We're here to help Katherine, remember?"

"That's right," I said, looking at her. She poked her lower lip out and studied the sidewalk. "What's the number of your father's building, Katherine?"

Without looking up, she answered, "It's the one with the blue awning across the street."

My eyes met Shel's. "You spotted it right away, didn't you?" he asked. She nodded silently.

"Why didn't you say so?" I asked.

"I'm afraid. I'm just . . . afraid."

"We can go home," Joyce said, patting her arm. "Don't worry, Katherine. Shel will—"

"Now just a minute," he interrupted. "Katherine, I risked our lives getting you here. Not to mention that if Mom finds out about this, she'll take the car away from me for a *year*."

Nudging Joyce, I joked, "In that case, we ought to tell Mom as soon as she gets home." No one smiled. "Sorry," I muttered.

"There's a phone," Shel said, pointing it out to Katherine. "We'll wait right here while you call him."

She raised her eyes to his face. Then she turned and walked slowly down the block toward the phone.

"Don't you think you were a little hard on her, Shel?" Joyce asked. "She's scared."

"Everyone is sometimes, babycakes," he said, ruffling her hair. "But after what she put us through, I don't think we should let her chicken out of this. If she wants to meet her father, fine. We've gotten her here. No better time than the present, right, Ab?"

"Right . . . except I've been standing here, trying to put myself in Katherine's shoes, like Mom is always telling us. I've tried, but I really can't imagine how it would feel to be looking up a father I've never met."

My twin's expression softened. Then he said, "We're right back to the same question: If this were you, would I let you chicken out?"

I snorted. "Fat chance."

He nodded. "Exactly."

"I don't care," Joyce said. "I feel bad for her."

"I do, too," I said, "but Shel's right, Joyce. If we really care about Katherine, we should treat her the way we treat each other. Maybe we've been too easy on her."

"Which is just as bad as being too hard on someone," Shel pointed out.

"Well, you better decide what to do now," Joyce said, sighing, "because here she comes, and she never made it all the way to the phone. I kept my eye on her."

No one said anything as Katherine walked up to us and stopped. "I've changed my mind," she announced, sticking out her chin.

"What does that mean?" Shel asked.

"I don't want to contact him. And you can't make me." She ducked.

Doubt flickered across Shel's face, but then he said, "Okay, so we'll go with you. We'll stay with you, too."

"Sure we will," I said. "We'll stick to you like glue, Katherine. You aren't alone."

"Do you promise?" she whispered.

I nodded just as Joyce tugged at my sleeve. "Maybe that's him!" She pointed at a man coming out of the building with the blue awning. The four of us stared as he walked quickly up the sidewalk. He wore a navy-blue golf shirt, khaki pants, and sneakers. There was a bald spot on the back of his head.

Turning to Katherine, I asked, "Do you think that's your father?"

"Abbey, how could I possibly *know?*"

"Look," said Sheldon, "it's almost one o'clock, and I'm getting hungry. Let's get this over with." He took Katherine's arm and started marching her across the street.

Just before we got to the curb, she pulled away from him, crying, "No! I'm not going to do it, and you can't make me!"

"That's what you think," Shel said. "Tell her, Ab. Tell her I have my ways."

When she looked at me, I shrugged, saying, "He is not above getting you in a headlock." Her hazel eyes grew round.

"Not to mention arm twisting," Shel said pridefully, "or hair pulling."

"My hair's too short to pull!" she snapped. Joyce started giggling. Katherine looked as if she might, too.

"Katherine," I said quietly, "you can't keep doing this to us."

Her face fell. "What have I done to you?"

"You can't keep doing whatever comes into your head with no regard to how it affects the rest of us," I explained. "When you're part of a family, you can't just do whatever you feel like."

"You had all of us running around in circles this morning," Shel chimed in. "And you've been moping around ever since your mother visited. Don't you realize how you make the people around you feel?"

"We know you're hurting, and it hurts us," I told her.

"The time has come to take action," Shel said, and cocked his head at me. "Ready?"

I nodded. Shel took one of Katherine's arms, and I took the other.

"Let me go!" she hollered. I think she might've stamped her foot, but we'd lifted her off the ground. Joyce brought up the rear as Shel and I carried our cousin up to the building with the blue awning.

We stopped in front of the apartment building. Under other circumstances I might have thought the doorman's pop-eyed expression, as he stared at us through the double glass doors, amusing.

"I can't do this," Katherine said breathlessly, pumping her feet in the air.

"Yes, you can," Shel contradicted. "Put her down, Ab." We put her down. "All you have to do is walk in there, give the doorman your name, and then ride the elevator up to your father's floor. Anyone can do that—even little Joyce here!"

"I'm not so little!" said Joyce.

"All right . . ." Katherine took a deep breath. "I *can* do it, but I don't want to."

"Then what do you want?" I asked.

"I don't know. Yes, I do." She lowered her head. "What I really want is to stay . . . with you."

"Why didn't you just *say* so, man?" Sheldon cried, and clapped her on the back. Fortunately, Joyce and

I had seen it coming and grabbed her to keep her from crashing to the sidewalk.

That was when the doorman opened the door and asked, "Can I help you?" in a tone that made it obvious that it was the last thing he wanted to do.

"No, thank you," Katherine answered, and quickly walked away.

Twenty-two

"Piece of cake," Shel bragged, pulling up in front of the house an hour or so later. "Home again the same day, right, girls? Man, that was a breeze!" He beamed at me, then at Joyce and Katherine in the backseat. Nobody said anything. We got out of the car.

As we went up the steps to the little dump on the hill, Joyce said, "I'm glad *that's* over."

"Me, too," I said.

"Well, I'm not," said Guess Who. "Man, that was great, motoring around in the Big Apple. Not bad, hey, Ab? Finding my way around the city and all."

"Not bad," I agreed, too drained to argue.

As soon as we got into the house, Katherine said, "I'm going to write to Claudia."

"Don't tell her about Shel taking the car," I warned. "No one says a word to Mom about this, either."

"Would she be angry?" Katherine asked.

"Sure she would," Shel told her. "Haven't you figured it out, yet, Katherine? Adults *freak* if you do the least little thing out of the ordinary. The less they know, the better, man!"

"No one's ever 'freaked,' as you put it, over any-thing I ever did," Katherine said, sounding forlorn.

"Really?" I asked.

"Really." She nodded.

"Well, those days are over," Shel told her. "You know, Katherine, you may not always like being part of this family."

"Why not?" she asked.

"Well, in addition to having to thwart Mom's ten-dency to be overprotective, we tend to be, ah, direct about things. We tend to insist that people tackle stuff instead of just sitting around complaining."

"I hate to admit it," I said, "but that was well put, Sheldon."

"No kidding, Ab." He breathed on his fingernails before polishing them on his sleeve. "So it's agreed. No one tells Mom about our little trip to New York.

"Hey, you girls," he said as the three of us started up the stairs. We stopped to look back at him. "Who's going to ask Mom to talk to Kevin about Katherine staying?"

"Maybe we all should talk to her," I said.

Katherine paled. "What if he doesn't want me? I don't think I could stand it if . . ."

Squeezing her hand, I turned to my brother. "Should we talk to Mom together, or do you want to do it alone, Shel?"

"Don't let him do it!" said Joyce. "You *know* he'll forget and start bragging about how he drove into New York."

"You're right," I said. "No way the golden boy could resist telling such a great story of daring."

"Now just a minute!" Shel snapped.

"I'll talk to Mom," I said. "Better yet, I'll sit down with Mom *and* Mr. Macartney—I mean, Kevin."

"Thank you, Abbey," my cousin said.

"Yeah," Joyce said, patting my shoulder. "Thanks a lot."

"You three don't have much confidence in me—even after what I did today," Shel sputtered.

"No offense," I said, "but you do suffer from diarrhea of the lip on occasion, Shel."

"Hey, face it. It's *tough* to be modest when you're as good as I am." Suddenly, he dashed up the stairs at us, laughing like the maniac he was.

"Whew!" Joyce gasped, slamming our bedroom door in the nick of time. "He almost caught us that time." She held the latch down, making it impossible for Sheldon to get in.

He pounded on the door, yelling, "No fair locking me out! And after everything I've done for you, too!"

"If you don't leave us alone," Joyce warned, "I'm telling Mom, and she'll never leave you in charge again."

There was sudden silence. A moment later, we heard him stomping down the hall to his own room. "You handled that perfectly, Joyce," I said.

"Thanks, Ab."

"Sometimes I feel sorry for Shel," Katherine said,

185

sitting down in the window seat. "It seems as if we're always excluding him."

"Fine," I said. "Open the door, Joyce. Tell Shel he can come in."

She started to protest, then rolled her eyes and opened the door. "You can come in, Shel," she called down the hall.

But just as he stepped into the cramped room, the phone rang. "I'll get it!" he hollered so loud that Katherine jumped.

As he galloped into Mom's bedroom across the hall, I turned to her. "Did you hear anyone else express the slightest interest in answering the phone?" I asked.

She put a hand over her mouth, giggling, shaking her head.

"Hey, dog face!" Shel yelled.

"Woof?" I yelled back.

He broke up laughing. "It's that weird friend of yours, Ab."

As I left the room, Joyce said, "He's so tactful." Katherine started laughing again.

Twenty-three

I bit my lip, eyeing myself in the bathroom mirror.

Today was the first day of school. My hair had grown long enough that I could almost tuck it behind my ears now. At this rate, it might be down to my collar by the time I graduated from high school.

When Katherine appeared behind me in the mirror, I wiped the mope off my face and winked at her. But she didn't smile.

"You look pretty," I said.

She smiled faintly. "Thanks. So do you."

"Sheldon, Abbey, Joyce, Katherine!" Mom yelled from downstairs. "Kevin just drove in. I want you down here, pronto!"

"Can you believe this?" I grumbled, taking a last swipe at my hair. "I'm a junior, and she's still taking first-day-of-school pictures."

"It's a first for me," Katherine said.

"And it's different this year, Ab," Joyce pointed out as she came out of our room.

"What's the difference, babycakes?" I asked as Shel joined us. The four of us fell into line and started down the stairs.

"This year Katherine's with us and Kevin's taking videos," she answered.

Mom beamed as she gave us a final inspection. "You're a sight for sore eyes," she murmured.

From the corner of her mouth, Katherine asked, "Is that good or bad?"

"Good . . . I think," I answered.

Mom laughed. "You kids go out and ask Kevin what he wants you to do," she told us. "I'll be out as soon as I can find the camera." She ran up the stairs, leaving the four of us in the dimly lit hall.

"All right, who's going first?" Sheldon asked.

"Don't look at *me*," I said.

"Or me," said Joyce. "After all, I'm the baby of the family."

"But I'm the cousin of the family!" Katherine protested, laughing as Sheldon took her by the arm and escorted her to the door. "I'm not even a Reilly!"

"All the more reason you should be the first victim," he said, and launched into ghoulish cackling. Then he whipped open the door and shoved her outside. "Terrific," he said, peering through a crack in the door. "Kevin's immortalizing Katherine having a giggle attack." Before I saw it coming, he cried, "Next!" and hurled me into the void.

"What do you want me to do?" I called. "Kevin, this is *embarrassing*."

"You're doing fine," he said, laughing uproariously. "Just keep making those faces, Abbey!"

Eventually, we were all out there, posed in front of

the little dump on the hill—our present and future home, I thought as Mom got into the act, snapping frame after frame on Dad's . . . I mean, *our* old camera. Naturally, Sheldon started acting like a pain, hamming it up, kissing us girls—when he wasn't putting horns behind our heads, of course.

The only thing that saved us was Don Champion speeding up the driveway in his father's car. He was giving Shel a ride to Fitchett Academy.

As soon as Shel and Don had left, we three girls said good-bye to Mom and Kevin and started down the driveway to catch the bus.

As we walked along under the trees, Katherine chuckled, saying, "That Shel. Do you think he'll ever grow up?"

"No," I answered. "At least I hope he doesn't . . . because when Shel grows up, it'll mean he's grown old."

"How do you mean?" Joyce asked, putting her hand into mine. This was one of the good things about my sister. She was still as affectionate as she'd been when she was little. I hoped it was one thing that would never change.

Looking up at the clear blue sky, I said, "I used to think Shel was hopelessly immature, the way he kidded around all the time, the way he harassed us. . . . But ever since you came to live with us, Katherine, I've realized it's more that he's young at heart, not immature. Look how he drove you into the city to visit your father. I couldn't have dealt with that situation the way he did. He just . . . took charge."

"Yes, he did. And he made you talk to Kevin, Abbey. Remember?" She smiled so that her whole face lit up. "If Shel had insisted that he talk to Kevin and Aunt Evelyn about me staying here, instead, you might still be calling Kevin Mr. Macartney."

"But Joyce was the one who said Shel would brag about driving into New York," I pointed out. "You're right, though. Talking to Mom and Kevin about you was the first time I treated Kevin like part of the family."

Katherine nodded, saying, "I think it was part of Shel's plan."

We reached the end of the driveway just as Joyce's bus came over the hill. "Bye, Ab," she said. She grinned at Katherine, adding, "Good luck."

"Thank you, *chérie*," Katherine said, giving her a hug. After waving until Joyce's bus was out of sight, Katherine turned to me. "How do I look? Do you think the other kids will make fun of me?"

"They didn't make fun of me when I was new last winter. You'll do fine," I said. "I don't worry about you for a . . ."

"What is it?" Katherine asked. "You have an odd expression on your face."

"I was just about to say, 'I don't worry about you for a minute.' Gram said that to me not long ago. I'd been telling her I was afraid. . . ."

"You?" She laughed. "When are you afraid, Abbey? You always seem so confident."

"Really?" I asked, pleased. "Brother, wait till I tell Sheldon you said that."

She laughed again. "It's wonderful," she said as our bus came over the hill.

"Riding the bus is wonderful?"

"No, no," she said as the bus pulled up. "It's wonderful the way you and Sheldon measure yourselves against each other. You two bicker, but you really care about each other."

As we boarded the bus, someone called, "Hi, Abbey! Dynamite haircut!"

"Thanks," I said. "My cousin did it. This," I announced to the bus at large, "is my cousin, Katherine Abernathy. She's living with us."

"For how long?" a boy asked, smiling at her.

"For . . . ever?" I shrugged.

My cousin's hazel eyes sparkled with laughter as she said gravely, "Or at least until I grow up."